MANAGING CHANGI

For a complete list of Management Books 2000 titles,
visit our web-site on http://www.mb2000.com

MANAGING CHANGE AT WORK

54 Approaches to Brickwall Management

Michael Wash

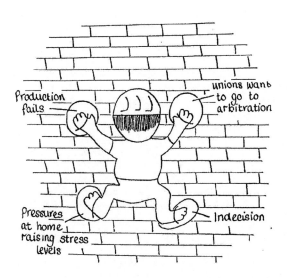

Text illustrations by Rebecca Snowdon

2000

First published in 2006 by Management Books 2000 Ltd
Forge House, Limes Road
Kemble, Cirencester
Gloucestershire, GL7 6AD, UK
Tel: 0044 (0) 1285 771441
Fax: 0044 (0) 1285 771055
E-mail: info@mb2000.com
Web: www.mb2000.com

Printed and bound in Great Britain by 4edge Ltd of Hockley, Essex
www.4edge.co.uk

British Library Cataloguing in Publication Data is available
ISBN 1-85252-521-5

978-1-85252-521-7

Dedication

To my Mother and Sister,
       both of whom died so tragically, yet their spirit lives on.

To my twin sons, Matthew and Thomas,
       whom I am so proud of and I love dearly.

To my step-children, Myles and Philippa,
       who have enriched my life significantly.

To my Wife, Mave,
       who continues to be my love, support and inspiration.

Contents

Contents

Preface

The stimulus for this book came through my own and others' experience with change – both reaction to change and the attempts to make change happen.

For the last twenty years, I have guided, counselled, implemented and resisted change. The many dynamics and effects of change, and methods of implementing it, are, I believe, worthy of illustrating in a language that can be related to and adopted worldwide. The prime focus of this book is for anyone who wants to make sense of change at work or just stay one step ahead; however, I recognise its application in all walks of life. I have tried to combine humour and cynicism with useful hints and serious messages.

Through its people, organisations of the future must quickly and effectively adapt to social and economical changes without sacrificing quality. Flexibility is increasingly seen as a positive attribute of a successful company. The excellent companies of the future will be served by a network of self-managing people, working on a basis of trust where **brickwalls** (resistance) are a rarity.

Change confronts us every hour of every day, whether awake or in our dreams.

Our brickwalls are a symbol for what stops us from changing.

It is important to know your own brickwalls as this will help you identify:

- your ability to adapt and change
- your limitations and strengths
- your reasons for protecting yourself.

Knowing your own wall will help you respect and handle others. Illustrated here are fifty-four approaches to managing resistance to change.

Use an approach that suits you and those around you. Discuss one that relates to relevant company or group issues.

I hope that you enjoy reading this book and that you are not constrained by narrow interpretations.

My intentions are to widen the whole area of change management by recognising the relevance of human reaction to change.

By entering into each situation and placing your own experiences and meaning into the words and illustrations, your sense of discovery will be enriched.

By the way, the Brickwall Management techniques read differently each time, that is, unless you're a brickwall, of course.

Happy dismantling.

Suggestions as to how you can use this book

1. Just read it and enjoy it. After reading the introduction, just dip into it from time to time.
2. Use it for personal self-challenge.
3. Apply your own experiences to the metaphor. Label the wall and strategy to deal with it.
4. Read it at the beginning of a meeting to help you focus on your own and your team's resistances and prejudices.
5. Just reading one of the approaches once may leave you confused. Better to read and ask yourself, or discuss with others, the following.
   a. In this case, who is the brickwall? Do you resist change in this way? Who do you know who wants change in these situations?
   b. Is this approach appropriate? How often have you seen it used – does it work? What is the cost and benefit of this approach?
   c. What are the values underpinning this approach? What personal and organisational issues does this discussion raise?
6. There are at least another fifty ways – but I'll leave them for you to discover.

Acknowledgments

Thanks to a group of colleagues, TD8, who were a leading-edge consultancy group in British Telecom. I have learnt a great deal from their expertise in change management.

Also, thanks to my boys, Matthew and Thomas, who constantly challenge my walls and remind me of my roots.

To Gerry Egan, Chris Argyris and Deepak Chopra whose work inspires me and gives me hope for organisational excellence through the transition from organisational structure change to a network of relationships which work with change to serve the customer, community and each other.

Also to Graham Higgins, Graham Dexter, Basil Youde, Mario Van Boeschoten, Tony Bell, George Buchanan, Graham Barkus and Chris Bunker, whose feedback and encouragement have been important to me.

And to the following organisations whose efforts to master change I admire – Cathay Pacific Airways and Royal Liverpool Children's Hospital NHS Trust.

Thanks to Caren, my PA and Office Manager, whose loyalty and support over the years has significantly contributed to our success.

Finally to Cliff Corrall, a great friend, a great man, rest in peace.

Why the Third Edition?

Change begins and is constant throughout my life. Understanding myself throughout change is my desire, yet so hard to do.

To accept my own personal pain as a gift and to recognise my own potential for learning during these times is a challenge, but worthy of celebration.

Letting go of the past and changing myself through the unknown, risks being lost and therefore I can only rely on myself as the guide – this is my hope.

Being conscious in every moment and being aware and responsible for my influence reminds me of my power.

Taking care of myself and being open to receiving creates opportunities for me to give.

I need to learn in order to change, being present and connecting this awareness to my desires for the future will enable me to move.

I can thrive on change and the change of others, for within this learning partnership I can see my worth and the worth of others.

My thirst for knowledge will surround me with books and help me strive for new experiences so I can listen and grow.

I value my tears as I know they are a path to joy.

I strive to listen more to my body so it doesn't have to shout so much.

I pray that what I write becomes real and that I live with a trust that gives me peace.

I wrote this in 1987 whilst I was having treatment for cancer. At the time, I was working for a large company and questioned: 'does it have to take a personal crisis for people to realise the importance of change?' Here lies the seed of this book.

Within this third edition are my thoughts behind each Brickwall management approach. I offer them to you with a dream and hope that 'work' becomes a place where we thrive, learn, develop, have fun and become fulfilled in knowing we are contributing in some small way to a better world.

Michael G Wash (2006)

Introduction

A guiding principle to carry you throughout your journey in Brickwall Management is:

Our walls are ourselves, and we all have an inner and an outer dimension of resistance.

Here are some examples:

Inner (statements about self)

- Lack of confidence.
- Perception of poor self-ability, lack of or inappropriate skill.
- Fear of the unknown.
- Familiarity and comfort in old ways of working.
- Security of past and present.
- Tiredness, stress, or other physical reasons for not changing.
- I like myself as I am.
- No need to change.
- If I change, what happens to the relationships I have?
- I'm too old for this game.
- I need more experience before the next step.
- I need to finish what I am doing first and learn from it before I try anything new.
- It's all too risky; I might fail or be rejected.
- I'm not senior enough to challenge the powers that be.

Outer (statements about others, or reasons given for not changing)

- This company is proud of its tradition and has built its reputation on solid and sound virtues.
- We need to be convinced of the operational value before risking new development.
- We have no confidence in the proposed changes or in its top-down imposition, and we are not involved, so we will continue to do our own thing.

- It costs too much money.
- Our priorities at the moment are productivity, shareholder satisfaction, and meeting deadlines, so don't talk about change now.
- The boss won't wear it.
- It may have worked there, but we are different.
- It's all been tried before.
- Interesting proposal – let me have more details before I decide whether to have a steering committee on this or not.
- Sorry, no resources.
- This is not your concern.
- I don't trust you.
- Do you realise the legal implications and complexities of this?
- At another time, this proposal would be very appropriate.

If any of this sounds familiar then read on. If not, give it to someone who has said 'no' to something new recently.

In order to help you choose the appropriate brickwall approach, it is advisable that you do some preparation.

Two principles of preparation to help you are:

1. know your brickwall

2. know yourself.

Preparation 1

➜ Know your Brickwall

Study its height, thickness and strength, *i.e. know the nature of resistance that faces you.*

When was it made? It may be important to know the state of the cement holding it together (e.g. if you choose to clamber over an old decrepit wall, it may collapse, hurting you in the process.) If you, or someone else, have been resisting something for a long time, then this needs to be respected; however this is not to say there is not a way around this old wall.

At what angle is it? Is it leaning? *i.e. what prejudice is contributing to the resistance?*

Does it have any peculiarities – barbed wire, glass, stakes or hidden traps? People have a need to protect themselves, usually because they have previously been hurt or let down, resulting in a low trust threshold.

What does the approach look like? Steady, unfocused or corrupt? (Experimenting with change and gaining early results can be difficult in a hostile or sceptical environment.)

What's the quality of the brickwall's surface? Where are its cracks and holes? What are the positive payoffs for the old system? Can you identify openings to be used positively?

Preparation 1 essentially involves self meditative exercise to look at your own willingness to change.

Preparation 2

➔ Know yourself

Different elements of this will be explained for certain approaches; however, there are some general principles to follow.

Personal development
- ✓ Believe in yourself.
- ✓ Use your powers of creativity.
- ✓ Recognise that you are only strong to the extent that you know your weaknesses.

Wall relationship (how you view yourself and others)
- ✓ Respect it.
- ✓ Is it serving a purpose?
- ✓ Timing is important, e.g. if you scale a wall at the wrong time, it's likely you will have misjudged its height; thus you will get tired and fall off! (Some willingness to change needs to be present).
- ✓ Don't believe what the wall says is on the other side. This is an old wall trick to distract you from your purpose – usually, it involves thoughts of self doubt.

Traditional, Less Effective Approaches

1. Talk at the Wall

(Talking is a poor relative to listening)

This requires considerable stamina and excellent verbal communication skills.

Use varying tone and pace to prevent boredom.

If talk persists, the wall may sag, and then you may need another approach to complete the breakthrough.

Have you ever been at one of those meetings where someone goes on and on, whether the response is strong argument or silence? It's amazing what checking understanding can do to help in these situations.

When faced with a Brickwall

When faced with someone talking at you for long periods of time - sit down, nod appropriately, and take notes if you want to. Try to listen to the core message not every word. Do not react. Eventually they will tire and realise you have something to say.

When *you* are the Brickwall

If you find yourself talking at people or dominating the discussion in order to persuade - then pause. You are probably anxious, wanting attention or need to control the situation. Better to slow down, listen more than talk. (2 ears, 1 mouth - so ratio of listening to talking should be 2:1)

2. Argue, Debate

(Emotional defence will beat rational attack)

Brickwalls are masters at withstanding logical and rational reasoning. Although this one may be useful for parliamentary candidate preparation and union official training, its effectiveness is limited as a method for breaking down defensiveness. This is partly because brickwalls are held together by strong emotions which are no match for rational argument.

When faced with a Brickwall

Some people will seem stubborn, unreasonable or obstinate. However, deep down - these people may have a strong emotional objection to your proposal. Therefore, try and understand and get them to describe what's really going on.

When *you* are the Brickwall

There will be times when a very strong and logical case for you doing something differently will be put to you - yet deep down, (your heart or guts) something tells you it's not right. This needs to be respected and explored. Try to find out what this source of discomfort is and describe it.

3. Scale the Wall

(Patience and willingness to get close can have its rewards)

This is one of the more successful strategies. Remember a brickwall is a symbol that represents your own resistance or resistance from others you want to change.

This approach requires good preparation, stamina and strength.

Preparation involves measuring the size of the wall, particularly its height. Researching the likely effect of your impact on it, may also give useful hints as to the best starting point. This will help you prepare both mentally and in choosing the appropriate equipment or resources necessary.

The advantages of this approach are with skill (you probably will need some training) you can fix your anchoring points by pulling yourself closer – those who are strangers to intimacy will find this particularly difficult – giving you more insight as to the nature of the wall.

This will help you decide where next to fix your point, pulling yourself up and securing progress as you go. You will also be celebrating insights about yourself and others as you climb.

The disadvantages include giving the wall time to detect weaknesses in your style and/or approach; this may dislodge a point. And there will be plenty of reflective moments for those old doubts to creep in.

This can be time consuming and, for some, a life-long task. However, learning gained through this approach is likely to put you in good standing for the future.

When faced with a Brickwall

> Do not underestimate the impact even a small change can have on others. So, step by step, get to know peoples' circumstances and fears. Reassure, shape and work with them until they 'own' and accept the need for change.

When *you* are the Brickwall

> Faced with a new situation, many of us are reluctant to rush in. Understandable, yes - ask yourself why? Do you know and trust the people proposing the change or know enough about the implications of the change? What's the risk? Do the benefits outweigh the negatives? Do you believe them? Sometimes it is better to embrace the unknown and let go of the familiar - it is then that real learning, surprise and fulfilment can be found.

4. The Suction Method

(Persistence and risk taking needed here)

You will need commitment to stick to it and not to let go. Eventually, at each point of suction – through the release of air and/or tension – the wall will allow you to release and progress upwards. Progress through the unknown can be a daunting task and at times there will be a temptation to stick with what you already have, rather than progressing further.

The dangers

● The wall may have considerable resistance to letting go; it's difficult to let go of long held beliefs, ideas, traditions, status and secure structures. You could be there for a long time: the shortest time for the average wall scaled is five minutes, and the longest (using this method) is a lifetime!

● This can be noisy and a drain on muscle power; it requires a willingness to ask for help and a commitment to keep going.

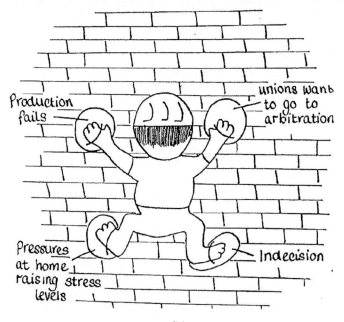

When faced with a Brickwall

People, systems, procedures - the way we have always done it! Things that have been around for a long time! These may take time to change. Communicate clearly what you are trying to achieve and why. Involve others; don't be afraid to ask for help.

When *you* are the Brickwall

Managing change or changing yourself can be a long and tortuous path. Persistence is a quality needed and aided with reminding yourself what you desire by this change. Pausing on the way, and reflecting and celebrating what you have achieved so far - can give you encouragement to move on.

5. Go Round the Wall

(Avoidance eventually leads to loneliness)

Advantages:

- Avoids conflict.
- Provides opportunity for exercise and discipline in stamina.
- Allows learning and discovery in many unrelated things.
- Gives time to think of alternatives.

Disadvantages:

- It's time consuming.
- When using this method, walls have an uncanny quality of mysteriously increasing in length, just as you think you are at its end.
- Can end up, after much effort, at the same place you started from.
- Can lose sight of original task and the wall appearing again at some unexpected time.

When faced with a Brickwall

People avoid things for all sorts of reasons. Being patient, offering reassurance and picking your time (when they are most receptive) to discuss the 'change' or issue. Try to understand the reason for avoiding as well as explaining the reason for change.

When *you* are the Brickwall

Have you ever felt yourself avoiding someone or an issue, or doing something new? You avoid because you imagine it will be difficult, painful or negative in some way. However, if you always do what you always do, you will always get what you have got! This is a recipe for 'status quo' or stagnation. People, things, relationships move on. Better to move with, rather than avoid - unless you want to be on your own, in the same place, always?

6. Convince the Wall It Doesn't Exist

(Saying it, doesn't mean you believe it)

You need to acquire the art of 'power speak', i.e. making statements with strength and conviction to the brickwall. For example:

- you are not appropriate
- you are not doing what you were designed to do
- your purpose is not important
- you have no foundations for being a barrier.

This method will work if:

- you believe in what you are saying
- you're honest with yourself, and you can celebrate your strengths and manage your limitations with support built in.

Cautions
- It can backfire if the wall rises to the challenge and your conviction is not there; then the wall can be reinforced (I know I shouldn't have done this).
- It usually needs the support of another method to increase the strength of your belief that it no longer exists.

When faced with a Brickwall

> Communicating with confidence, belief and commitment is necessary if you are to win over those who are just fearful of change. Do this with heart-felt passion and at the same time, reassure those who come with you that they have your support and you have a chance.

When *you* are the Brickwall

> Your imagination can be both your friend and foe. Personal barriers or blocks to doing something are all in your imagined self, ie: it hasn't happened, it's in the future so is still in the category of fantasy. The fear and anxiety is real, but the event isn't. Equally, you could imagine no barriers or blocks and experience your fears dissipate and your confidence rise.

7. The Holiday Option

(Go for the right reasons)

This usually occurs when reasons for brickwallness are put down to stress, overwork, and tiredness (brickwall 'fired out').

It can be the case that the holiday option is appropriate; however, many mistakes are made in this area.

- Sending her, him or the wall on holiday with high stress and unresolved issues can cause further stress – fears related to not being in control and being dispensable.
- The time off may reinforce brickwallness and return them firmer and more steadfast. The holiday can unintentionally be seen as a reward for appropriate pre-holiday behaviour.
- The changes made in the individual's or the wall's absence makes things harder to adjust to on return.

So, use the holiday option only as a last resort. If it is to be used – careful briefing and debriefing need to be made.

When faced with a Brickwall

Tempting to send them away for a while and implement the change in their absence. This will only build in mis-trust - better to openly discuss than avoid the issue.

When _you_ are the Brickwall

Going on holiday, or being sent on holiday/leave because your stress is seen as blocking progress – not a good frame of mind to be away in. Better to work with those concerned and take structured time-out to reflect on the reason for stress and resistance. Try to resolve these before you take a break or you will only be carrying them around as baggage for the whole holiday.

8. Give the Wall a Reading List

(Reading when you are searching for answers is most effective)

This one is for the academics who believe in change through knowledge acquisition. It is effective when you have gained the attention and interest of the brickwall by giving relevant quotes and references. You need to speak with conviction and enthusiasm about the personal insights gained through reading, e.g. 'this one changed my life!'

Ideally, respond to the brickwall's request, 'Have you got anything I can read on this?'

You can also, especially in a power position, give mandatory reading. This is likely to work for those walls who aspire to greater things like a building. (e.g. 'I want to be like you, boss, so I can force people to read too'). This is not usually effective unless backed up with a clear, practical outcome.

When faced with a Brickwall

Making resistance to change discussable by asking people to read a book on the subject can work as long as you follow it up and are prepared to receive feedback as to what's really going on.

When *you* are the Brickwall

When faced with someone talking at you for long periods of time, be open to the possibility that there will always be something new to learn that will be of personal benefit to you. Start reading with an enquiring mind - start with a question, e.g. how do others cope with change? Then search for an answer through reading - it doesn't have to be academic or theory - pick most novels or fairy tales and 'managing change' will jump out at you if you hold the question.

9. Ignore the Wall

(You still know it can get in the way)

This is one for the patient and disciplined. Before embarking on this method, assess the cost in terms of the time it will take in relation to the cost of not having what the wall is trying to block. This technique is based on the behavioural principle of ignoring negative behaviour, looking for signs of movement and reinforcing any movement positively.

The small and simple rewards are usually the least used and most effective. A formula to help is:

1. Highlight the positive.

2. Say why it is important and indicate the value of the contribution.

3. Praise with thanks, and if appropriate, reward with something more tangible.

When faced with a Brickwall

> If you were faced with 50 people denying or resisting change, and 50 people who were positive - where does the attention go?
>
> Concentrate on the 50 positive! 'Attend to the flowers and the weeds will die.' Demonstrate the power and beauty of change - most of the others will follow.

When _you_ are the Brickwall

> Denying the inevitable may buy you time, but eventually, you will have to realise that you can only change those things you have some control over. In this case, your feelings and reactions to the change you face.

10. Distract and Pass

(Don't put off till tomorrow what you can do today)

Common methods under this approach include:

● keeping it busy with urgent work that requires its attention

● complimenting it on its strength and asking for support to do something it is likely to be interested in – with direct involvement and some movement. (Have you ever caught yourself being very busy, yet you know there is something you are avoiding or not facing up to?)

Caution

This may work in terms of passing; however, you should be prepared for the wall closing back and calling in help from other walls and trapping you in a very difficult situation. (Procrastination is one of the brickwall's greatest friends.)

When faced with a Brickwall

'I'm too busy'. If this is the reason you are getting for not progressing in new activities, then have a discussion about priorities. What's important for you, the team and the organisation? Then explore what's really going on and offer support.

When *you* are the Brickwall

Being busy, and putting off till tomorrow what you could do today, can be a way of avoiding things that are seen as difficult or uncomfortable. It is sometimes better to take a walk and/or reflect on the question: what is really important here?

11. The Writing is on the Wall

(Listen carefully to the messages around you)

Get closely involved with what is inevitably going to be significant change. Point out the signs, signals and clues.

Make predictions, i.e. 'If you continue to stand there, this is what will happen.' Draw a solution-effect diagram starting with the brickwall and looking at the consequence of not shifting.

Give it space to look at itself from a different angle, or at least stand back a little. Give people the time and opportunity to see themselves in action.

If this is done in a helpful manner and used in combination with Brickwall Management Approach (BMA) 12, this can be effective; however, if it is done with negative confrontation, i.e. with open criticism and humiliation, then reinforcements to its foundations are likely.

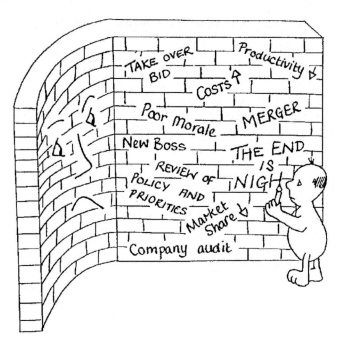

When faced with a Brickwall

Present the options - no change, carry on as we are - this will happen. Alternatively, if we change this way, we can achieve this . . . . Give them a choice - risky huh?

When *you* are the Brickwall

Sometimes, you are just too close or wrapped up in your own world to see what's happening all around you. Don't be a victim - be a partner, wake up and smell the coffee - stand back, read what's on the wall.

Traditional Effective Approaches

12. Positive Challenge

(Celebrate your strengths)

This involves skills that help the wall see its own weaknesses by reflecting back strengths (e..g. 'How is it that you use all of your strength to keep yourself rigid and immovable instead of using some of it to open up a little?')

Mirror techniques have been known to be successful – reflecting back accurately the meaning of what has been said – and will enable people to see themselves more clearly.

Additional preparation is required to carry on the life-long questions: 'What makes my reflections true for others?'

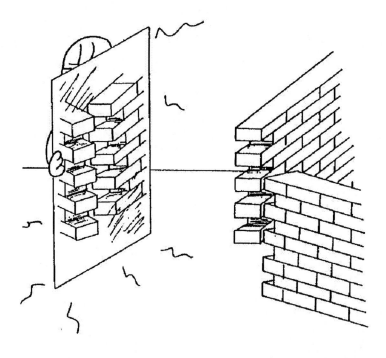

When faced with a Brickwall

> Listen carefully; demonstrate that you understand by reflecting back what you have heard. Listen to strengths and highlight these in a way the individual (or group) can apply them to the new situation.

When *you* are the Brickwall

> Take a good look in the mirror, what do you see? Try and see the miracle of you, your strengths, what you have achieved - and celebrate your uniqueness. Remind yourself that you have got where you are today by changing - celebrate and look forward to more change!

13. Help from Friends

(Open up and receive)

Friends fall into three major categories:

1. The long standing friends whose advice is often tolerated and listened to.
2. The work-related friends who are keen to impress and possibly need you more than you need them.
3. Recent friends or acquaintances whose help must be taken at face value. They must be filtered because although they may be well intentioned, the help or advice they give may be based on very little knowledge of you and your situation.

Help from friends is likely to be:

- Well-meaning advice – 'It seems that what you should do is …'
- Hard-hitting challenge – 'It's not like you to lose courage easily.'

- Gentle nudges or words of support – 'It's okay; I'm with you in whatever way you choose.'
- Showing you the way – 'Looks easy, I'll show you.'
- Misplaced advice – 'If I were you, I'd just get on with it; it hurts me to see you like this.'

42

Useful principles:

- Managers as advisors create a dependent workforce that usually needs more managers.
- Managers as agents of change, who help others solve their own problems, create an independent and a self-managing workforce.

When faced with a Brickwall

Misplaced advice from the boss is not a good idea. Better to ensure people have all the information available then give them the support to make an informed choice.

Learn how to coach others to solve their own problems and manage change.

When _you_ are the Brickwall

By all means, listen to your friends, but at the end of the day, you will have to take your own advice. Enjoy the attention you get from genuine friends, learn to receive love and affection. If this is what you want then you must also give it. What you pay attention to will grow.

14. Help from Things

(Look around and use what's available to you)

Things are a form of resource that can be utilised for overcoming barriers or reducing resistance to change.

There are many types of things, ranging from objects and nourishment to money. There are three steps to resource management:

1. Identify the type of resource needed.

2. Acquire it (even beg if you have to or borrow it.) *

3. Appropriately position and utilise your resources.

    * Beware not to overlook the fact that you may already have it.

When faced with a Brickwall

Faced with many excuses why things shouldn't change? Lack of time, resources or ability? Then remind them that there are at least 54 ways to find the things they need to be successful. Look around you, you are probably under-utilising the things/resources you currently have.

When _you_ are the Brickwall

If you hear yourself saying any of the following: 'I don't have the time', 'I'm too old', 'I haven't the confidence' or 'I have no resources' - then stop and take a look at what you do have. Your talents, your network of relationships, your potential. Most of us under-utilise our abilities by 80%, ie: we only use 20% of our innate intelligence, body and mind. Just tap into some of this and it's amazing what you can achieve.

15. Undermining

(Being underhand eventually will hurt you as well as others)

This is appropriate for a small team who prefer to work closely and intimately or in the dark.

- The wall may collapse on top of the team, causing severe damage and chaos.
- These teams often fall into an air of false security, not realising how visible they are.
- The teams tend to increase rumours and suspicions, adding strength to the wall.
- This requires a good sense of direction and clear communication to others, particularly those who have similar ideas. This can cause overlap and 'tunnel collapse'.

- Teams that are too busy attending to their own needs at the expense of business requirements, e.g. communication, strategy and results, are likely to experience a cave-in of their neatly channelled tunnels!

When faced with a Brickwall

Sometimes, when individuals or teams are left to their own devices too long, they build up defences to protect their own comfort zone. Better to ensure tasks are varied and, occasionally, completely change what they are doing. Lock them out of their office, get them to walk around!!

When *you* are the Brickwall

Whether you work on your own or in a team; if you become too inward looking, too preoccupied with your own work or team relationships, then you run the risk of 'working in the dark', oblivious of the changes going on without you, outside. Better to come up from 'under the ground' or out of the office, take a deep breath and really observe how the world around you changes with effortless ease.

16. Train the Wall to do something different – Send It on a Workshop

(How can you learn?)

This is one of the more commonly used methods. Workshops can be viewed differently depending on one's own beliefs and how the training is set up.

Positive Aspects

✓ Allows for investment in own people and brickwalls.
✓ Provides opportunity to learn new things and take a fresh look at the work environment.
✓ Allows him / her / it to get out of the way for a while, making things easier.
✓ Gives time to reflect and stand back from the situation and increases chance of choosing appropriate Brickwall Management Approach (BMA).

Negative Aspects

✘ Avoids the 'issue', putting the problem onto someone else.
✘ Makes training unrelated to needs.
✘ Often provides little follow-up to put learning into practice.
✘ May overcrowd brain-space with irrelevant knowledge.
✘ Fills drawer space with thick, unused files of training material.

To increase the positives and reduce the negatives, search for training that offers 'tailor-made', needs-based learning, experience and follow-up. Search for one that uses work-related issues and encourages utilisation of local resources.

The availability is limited and initially expensive, but it is cost-effective in terms of results.

When faced with a Brickwall

Ask the person you are sending on a training event/ workshop/conference before they go:
- Do you understand why you are going?
- Do you understand what it is about?
- Do you know what you want out of it?

Ask the person after the event:
- How did you get on?
- What were the main learning points for you?
- How can 'we' help you put this new learning in practice?
- … and let's book a follow up date to check how you are getting on.

When _you_ are the Brickwall

Have you ever found yourself on a workshop or training event and felt, or thought, that it is a waste of time? Whose responsibility is it, do you think, to learn? Time out of the work situation is always valuable. Even if the content or the trainer is not the best, you can utilise the time, space and your fellow learners to ask, 'What are my development needs?' and 'How can I improve?'

17. Just Rewards

(What motivates you?)

Build on BMA Number 9; reinforce all positive movement. Also, help set realistic goals. For many, going from a solid, proud and firm structure to a pile of rubble in one day is too much. Plan in steps and milestones and indicate the rewards related to each.

Do not underpay – be sure you recognise valuable contributions to future-orientated changes that even the most stubborn of walls can make.

Be creative in your reward and recognition policy – make visible and congratulate the change you want to happen.

When faced with a Brickwall

Be clear about your expectations regards new behaviours and competencies then reward and recognise those that begin to demonstrate these. There are at least 54 ways to recognise people, start with thanks then graduate to a full system of recognition and praise culture.

When *you* are the Brickwall

Why do you work, what motivates you - is it only the money? No matter what you are paid, everyone wants to work in a happy environment. One where your talents and skills are put to best practice and you get recognised for a job well done, i.e. occasionally somebody says 'well done and thanks'! If you are cynical (which, by the way, is 'love gone sour') and unhappy - change it! You can't change the pay policy - you can change how you feel and behave.

18. Group Pressure

(Teamwork can facilitate change)

Enforced results can be achieved if you lock a team in a room and release them only when consensus is achieved.

Scale of success through consensus	Success factor
1. Gives in quickly	Low
2. Gives in after a fight	Low
3. Gives in after a long, hard struggle	Low to minor change
4. Gives in when other's viewpoint is seen	Minor change
5. Is able to see and understand others rationale, so gives in	Some change
6. Feels listened to, so some others begin to see opposite view	Good chance of real change
7. Feels fully listened to and appreciated.	High chance of successful change
(Also confident that the others can see and respect the opposite view. Chooses to go with the majority for consensus, giving appropriate reasons)	

Useful hints

Consensus is rarely fully achieved. It is often skipped over by silence or slight nodding – which usually means that everyone doesn't fully agree, but it is easier to simply say 'yes'. A better alternative is to find a way of working which respects others' differences.

When faced with a Brickwall

Sometimes it is easier to just tell the team to get on with it, decision made - wrong! You will not get full commitment and motivation will be short lived. Better to go through the pains of listening to every group member's views about the way forward until a genuine consensus can be found, or at least difference of opinion acknowledged and taken into consideration. Do not take for granted the 'silent nodders' - they may need encouragement to speak out.

When *you* are the Brickwall

Ever been in a situation where you have thought it easier to go with the majority view as there are too many thinking differently from you? Here you must decide - is this (your brickwall) you being stubborn, or do you need to (as in number 2. Argue, Debate) describe your discomfort and feelings? Agreeing because others agree is not genuine agreement. It's false - and the consequences of this could create resentment and more resistance in you in the long run. Have the courage to be different and speak up.

19. Promote the Wall

(What do you want to be when you grow up?)

This is sometimes referred to as *'removing the obstacle by changing its responsibilities or role'*.

This unfortunately is a 'saving face' measure and is sometimes dressed up as promotion. Underestimating the insight and judgement of others in this situation is a mistake. The effect of this on the perception of those around is:

'It's okay to be a brickwall.'
'Brickwalls get rewarded.'
'Now I know what to do to get on.'

However, increasing its responsibility in the area of desired effect can cause positive change through personal conflict (i.e. if a manager disagrees with a programme, give him a significant portion of it to manage and eventually the manager will either start to think positively about it or break away all together). This will only work with that group of managers whose ability to self-challenge is recognised.

When faced with a Brickwall

In absence of a robust personal performance management system, you will get tolerance of poor performance and poor performers passed from one project or department to another. This is very expensive - better to invest in an appraisal system that is clear, fair and gives individuals a chance to improve.

When _you_ are the Brickwall

This is a difficult one to believe, but sometimes, people are moved on to a different job or promoted rather than confront the fact that you just do not 'fit' the demands of the current position. When moving job or career, ask yourself, whose choice is this? If it's yours for positive reasons - fine! If it's someone else's decision - then you run the risk of taking you, or the brickwall, with you - i.e. repeating the same patterns and mistakes. Better to dismantle before you leave, e.g. an honest review of your experience/performance so far.

20. Sack the Wall

(Better to admit failure than to struggle on with stress)

This is really a 'failure activity' when resorting to this, especially without trying the many other approaches available. However, there are some situations where this can be appropriate. If no movement takes place after the warnings and support to change, then 'the sack' may have to happen. Ideally at the time of dismissal, an air of acceptance on the wall's behalf is preferred, but this is rare and a fight for justice may ensue. The financial cost of constructive dismissal may be small compared to continuation of employment, however, there may be considerable human costs and hidden financial losses due to the deterioration of trust, motivation and publicity. If ever you catch yourself threatening someone with 'the sack', listen, because you're also threatening yourself with failure.

A quote to remember:

'A person who is genuinely and legitimately surprised by his or her annual performance appraisal provides grounds for dismissal of the person's boss.'

Tom Peters, *'Thriving on Chaos'*, Handbook for Management Revolution, London:
Macmillan, 1987

When faced with a Brickwall

Dismissing someone is the last resort. It should not come as a surprise to the person concerned as they ideally should have had every chance for development and performance review up to that point.

Using threat will only generate fear, defensiveness and reduce the opportunities for learning and improvement.

When *you* are the Brickwall

If you are ever in the unfortunate position of being sacked (dismissed) or threatened with the sack, then it should come as no surprise. If it does, then something has gone seriously wrong with your relationship with the boss, or you have underestimated the significance of a decision you are responsible for or the impact of your behaviour.

a) You either 'take it on the chin', count your losses, let it go and move on

b) Fight it, disagree, take to court, stand up if you feel you have been unfairly dismissed

c) Plead for a last chance, genuinely review your position, and commit to learning, development and regular performance reviews.

21. Redeployment

(Are you sure this is the job for you?)

Effectiveness of this approach will depend on:

    a. reason for redeployment
    b. method of redeployment, i.e.
- communication process
- counselling support
- support for options becoming available.

Ideally involve the person/brickwall in the decision for redeployment, so full understanding and credit for the decision can be achieved. However, practical and timely information can not always be communicated face-to-face. Support to work through the personal implications of redeployment is needed. A common mistake occurs

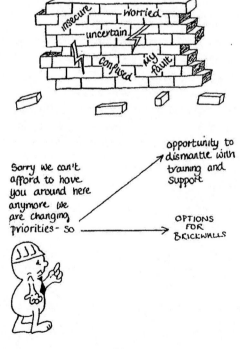

when decisions are made from the top, and very little effort is made to communicate down the chain the rationale behind the decisions.

At the end, the people are left having to change the job and, often, their lives. If family and location are involved, they resent the decision, and this reduces moti-vation and trust and increases their need for reinforcing the brick-walls around them.

This can be highly successful if an attitude of 'this is a new opportunity and chance to learn new skills' can be created. Development Centres and retraining opportunities are important support activities for this attitude.

When faced with a Brickwall

> Don't underestimate the significance of changing someone's job profile and/or location. Giving a clear and justified reason with good support options such as expenses and re-training are basic needs.

When _you_ are the Brickwall

> It can be a bit of a shock when faced with change of job and/or location. You can choose to resist, argue against, feel anxious or even be angry - or you can use it as an opportunity for a fresh start with new opportunities, learning and new relationships. The more positive you are, the more chance of your seeing the support options around you and the more willing people will be to help.

22. Redundancy

(Can you let go of what is familiar?)

Enforced redundancy is always a dramatic step, and for some, it is life threatening – especially if options are few.

However, it can be seen as:

✓ *'The best thing that ever happened to me.'*
✓ *'A new start with decent financial start up.'*

Again, the effectiveness of this will depend on how the decision is communicated and the quality of support available through financial and skilled counselling.

The need for the redundancy to be business-related, rather than expedient or personal is essential. Businesses have been known to spend more on hiring people back as consultants as a dearth of skills is brought about as a result of the redundancy programme!

When faced with a Brickwall

Offering redundancy to people because they refuse or are unable to change is inappropriate. Changing people's job to the extent that they are unable to fulfil it, then dismissing them, could be construed as constructive dismissal. Open and clear communication needs to be backed by a clear plan of support for those affected if you are going to maintain a positive image, reputation and the goodwill and motivation of those remaining.

When *you* are the Brickwall

Facing redundancy need not always be bad news, although invariably it comes as a shock. This is not personal rejection - it means the organisation has changed and the job no longer exists. It is a major shock to your 'brickwall' type characteristics as it is enforced change. However, it is hoped that you get some financial and development support to ease your transition into another job elsewhere.

Creative Approaches

23. Acquire Ghost-like Qualities

(Believe in your personal power)

This process requires some mental preparation.
A method of preparation is meditation using the TUFF chant.

→ I am **T**ransparent
→ I am **U**nstoppable
→ I am **F**lexible
→ I am **F**righteningly determined

Twenty minutes each day spent focussing on these qualities can significantly increase your belief and confidence in your potential. This is a challenge to make you believe in your own personal potential and spiritual quality of persistence.

When faced with a Brickwall

Sometimes, people need reminding that they are capable of a lot more than they realise. The only difference why some can walk on hot coals and others can't is their beliefs. Help them change 'yes, but ...' to 'yes, and ...', and remind them to highlight the positives in themselves, others or projects. Explain the benefits of thinking of solutions, not only problems.

When _you_ are the Brickwall

If you are someone whose 'glass is half empty', often replies to peoples' suggestions with a 'yes, but ...' or often looks at the negative before the positive - then you are likely to be seen as a barrier for others and will reduce your opportunity for happiness. Better to believe you have significant power and potential to glide through obstacles with ease. Stop having self-limiting beliefs and acknowledge your strengths and talents, and look forward to your growth with excitement.

24. Hypnotise the Wall

(False sleep makes it difficult to dream)

This is very effective in the short term.

The two main methods

1. Dazzle it with brilliance and complexity and then, when an altered state of consciousness is achieved through confusion, ask it to move.

2. Relax it into a false sense of security, then ask questions aimed at finding weaknesses to be used at a later date.

This method is more effective with recently built walls, and it is more difficult with walls established.

By using this method you may be accused of manipulation, as it often requires some element of trust to gain the hypnotic state.

In the long run, this method nearly always backfires, and genuine trustworthy relationships become difficult to find.

Sagging in the middle due to being relaxed

rugged, shaken at the edge due to confusion

54 Ways of being friends with brickwalls

When faced with a Brickwall

There is nothing wrong with making a powerful, passionate and stimulating presentation. It can be highly entertaining and motivational. However, if the sting in the tail is to get immediate buy-in, full commitment there and then - you need to recognise that this maybe short term, by people being carried away with the appeal. Challenge yourself - to what extent is your own ego (e.g. personal need for power and status) playing a part here? Better to let people think about proposals and to come back with questions and concerns and work through them together.

When *you* are the Brickwall

Sometimes, when faced with very eloquent and powerful speakers making suggestions to you about ideas that sound good - it can have a hypnotic effect - i.e. you glaze over, you can't understand the complexity but you are taken in with the speakers' passion. This is one situation where your Brickwall qualities can help out. Better to stand back, buy some time, reflect on the proposals in the cold light of day or you could end up buying into something without fully appreciating the implications.

25. Take the Wall to the Science Fiction Movie (World Without Brickwalls)

(Be creative)

This is one of a number of methods used to stimulate imagination and, in so doing, creating vision and strategy.

Effects:

- reduces inhibitions
- releases imaginative and creative resources
- gives clarity to what the future could be like
- increases chance of outcomes being more specific
- increases commitment to reduce brickwallness in business and life.

Be aware of (but don't be put off by):

- onlookers who may be envious and may accuse you of having your head in the clouds or having an unrealistic 'pie in the sky' attitude
- your own inhibitions through the 'yes, but. . . .' syndrome.

You would be better off with someone who knows the firm's 'script' and your personal 'script' to help you put into practice the insights gained. (Your script is your way of doing things – a well rehearsed dialogue that probably needs to change if new performance levels are to be achieved.)

This method is highly recommended for people who are truly stuck.

When faced with a Brickwall

It's easy to get stuck into routine. It's safe and comfortable to do the same things over and over again. However, this does not encourage growth and performance improvement. There is a direct correlation between breakthrough in thinking, new levels of performance and the degree of creativity. Have a 'wild thinking day', give prizes for the craziest ideas, encourage lateral thinking, promote puzzles and games to stimulate new ideas.

When *you* are the Brickwall

Instead of losing sleep over what might be and being reluctant to take risks - pause and reflect. Write down what you want. What do you desire in life - list the top 5 things. Once you have identified these, you can start listing at least 54 ways of achieving them - be creative. Imagine, if you had all the resources and health you want - what would you choose to do? If you are doing it now, then you have dream fulfilment.

26. Disguise the Wall

(Others may see you before you see yourself)

Make a permanent fixture. Admire it and reinforce the belief that it's justified in being a brickwall in disguise – that it is a good idea to change its name to 'just one of those things' or 'that's life' or 'it has always been there'.

This method can actually serve a genuine purpose, and it may only be a matter of time before the disguise comes off. Some people need to carry their disguises or brickwalls with them as a way of protecting themselves from the chaos around them.

This needs to be respected; however, some disguises are blatantly obvious and even silly, and the brickwall may actually appreciate being told this (in a sensitive and skilful way, of course).

When faced with a Brickwall

Challenging someone's beliefs and patterns of behaviour is very powerful. In this case, pointing out the obvious may be cruel to be kind, but at the end of the day - what do you want your epitaph to be? *'A reliable steady worker'* or *'Someone who made a difference and had fun doing it too!'*?

or ... Can you imagine doing the same thing day in, day out until you retire?

or ... Carry on like this; it will get you exactly where you are today!

When _you_ are the Brickwall

It may be that you have done the same thing for years and you and others have just got used to it, accepted it and never even thought of your doing anything else. Occasionally, along comes someone perhaps you don't know so well, who asks the simple questions:

'Have you always done this? Why?'

'Have you ever thought of doing anything else?'

They may even offer an observation - how sad to think that's all there is.

27. Find the Wall a Guru

(Learn from the wisdom of others)

This is suitable for those people or processes who have recognised brickwallness in themselves and have embarked upon a path of development to 'un-brick' themselves. It is important to learn the wall's purpose of being there in the first place, replacing it with wisdom, humility and love for both brick and non-brick elements. It is difficult to find a guru, as they are often inconspicuous. They may be the least expected people in the office. It's amazing who you can learn from, but it does require a degree of respect for the individual's experience and ability to listen on your behalf.

The guru and brickwall working together are only as effective as the degree of 'give' in the wall. If there is none at all, then the combination of the wall's stubbornness with the guru's respect could lead to a long, unchanging relationship.

When faced with a Brickwall

Guru may sound a little grandiose, but the principle of learning from someone who has wisdom to pass on is sound. Creating learning partnerships in your organisation (or life) can increase support and confidence in putting new learning into practice. Mentoring, shadowing and action learning are examples of this in practice. By the way, how are you seen in the organisation? Who looks up to you? Are you able to pass your wisdom on with humility?

When *you* are the Brickwall

When you feel stuck, sometimes turning to the words, life and wisdom of great men and women can help put things in perspective and / or give you inspiration. Who do you respect and why? What makes them a guru, leader or significant person? What have they achieved? How do they create or manage change? Read, reflect, and apply what makes sense to you.

28. Getting Back to Roots

(Never lose a sense of humility)

This is sometimes referred to as encouraging regression, asking, 'Where did all this start?'

Can you remember your first experience of putting up the wall, barrier or reason for not changing?

Helping the wall identify its own biography may give it insights to its 'raison d'etre' – the significant experiences that have contributed to present-day thinking. These are the links from natural elements to foundation and building; small edge walls to major constructions can often be incongruous and unrelated to the original intention for wall building in the first place.

Creative ways of encouraging wall regression are needed. This is a powerful technique and care is needed, or moisture will build up rapidly in the wall until it crumbles. However, a tearful response from managers can be very therapeutic, as it helps release tension and stress from things that may have been building up for years.

When faced with a Brickwall

Some people hold on to events or things that have hurt them for years. They build up defences to protect themselves from this happening again. Asking questions direct, such as *'have you always been this defensive, cynical or stubborn?'* may get you a defensive response. However, exploring what you might have in common and discussing the core purpose of why you are here may find that you have more in common than you think.

After all, wouldn't we rather be happy at work, knowing we are making a contribution and if we can have fun as well, then it begins to get easier - as natural as child's play.

When *you* are the Brickwall

Can you remember when you were carefree, fun-loving, without inhibition and really happy? Most people will recall happy times as a child. Some people manage to be like this in adult life. Is it possible to recreate some of these qualities in ourselves? What do you want, what have you got to lose?

Giving praise, recognition and best wishes to others, smiling a bit more, and seeing the joy in other people's lives will start to change people's reactions to you. We are all connected and part of the same family who, given a chance, would love to play and be happy together.

29. Make It Obsolete

(Sometimes, pointing out the obvious is all that is needed)

Build many other brickwalls, making the point that, in comparison, the original barrier is inconsequential. This, however, is a negative approach, and it is best handled hypothetically to help the wall gain insight before actually building other brickwalls. For example, use the statement, *'If we were all like you, this is what this business would look like'*.

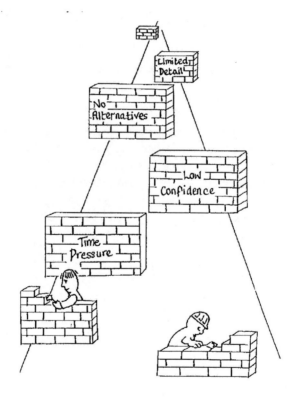

When faced with a Brickwall

Difficult one - as you may have that individual who, for years, has given good and loyal service, but is still holding on to old ways, which increasingly are becoming obsolete. Gently bringing this person into the 21st Century is the challenge, at the same time as respecting what they have achieved. Don't overlook the fact that they may be representing core values on which the business was based.

When _you_ are the Brickwall

Look around you - are you different for the right or wrong reason? Right - you contribute something of value that adds to the creative end result. Wrong - you are living in the past - some may call you a dinosaur. Do you want to become extinct, or do you want to get with the times? Find out what others are doing, what makes them tick, have a go - you never know - you might have some fun!

30. Brainstorm

(Go wild, let your ideas flow)

Brainstorm at least fifty-four reasons why we shouldn't be like a brickwall.

The principles of brainstorming

- Encourage the free flow of ideas.
- Write down everything said.
- Don't make judgements about others' ideas.
- Encourage the wild ideas, too.
- Work one-on-one or in groups.
- 'Piggy back' with others' ideas in a group and encourage anything else.
- Don't be constrained by writing materials.
- Ideally, 'use the wall'!

When faced with a Brickwall

Don't underestimate the skill to run an effective brainstorming session. You need to encourage the free flow of ideas, not just by technique but also by your attitude and behaviour. Just the slight negative overtone showing through in your tone of voice or body language will suppress the creative ones in your team. Be positive, give them genuine permission.

When *you* are the Brickwall

Ever have a problem and, once the problem is clear, the solution is obvious? You are likely to go for the first solution you think of. Don't. Give yourself the luxury of listing out at least 54 ways to solve the problem and I guarantee there will be a better solution to the first one you thought of. If you get the permission to 'brainstorm' - then go for it - don't hold back, all ideas are acceptable.

31. Encourage the Wall's 'Child'

(Be spontaneous – have fun)

Within each one of us, there still lie the qualities of the small child we once were. These are predominantly inconsistent with the brickwall qualities.

Encouraging play, humour, adventure and experimentation may help us to unlock the rich, creative potential that lies in all of us. Through imaginative play, we find ways of opening up. Taking a team outside of its familiar surroundings can encourage these qualities.

Also, ponder the question, *'How is it that some may see the following as a hat whilst others may see it as a boa constrictor digesting an elephant?'*

Antoine de saint Exupery, Antoine
The Little Prince, London: Pan Books, 1945

When faced with a Brickwall

If you have a team who feel inhibited for whatever reason - take them out of the work surrounding, create an event where they can be themselves - then debrief the event and ask: *'what would it take to recreate the fun and spontaneity at work?'*, *'what changes would we have to commit to?'*

When _you_ are the Brickwall

When was the last time you did anything spontaneously, i.e. without pre-thought or planning? Tap into your intuition, go with your feelings and experience the result. You will be surprised at the result. It may give others permission to do likewise and, before you know it, you and your team/ colleagues are enjoying the whole experience.

Desperate Approaches

32. Blow the Wall Up

(Never too late to diffuse the situation)

This is a drastic step, usually a sign of desperation on behalf of the manager. Often it is accompanied by feelings of hatred and accusations of the wall throwing bricks; thus it justifies the use of explosives. This situation can occur as a result of escalating conflict when people start talking in terms of 'beating the other side' and 'pulling one over' or 'no way am I going to lose.' Immediate input in negotiation skills is required here, so a move to a 'win-win' situation can be achieved.

When faced with a Brickwall

When you get to a stage where you just want to destroy the opposition, you have already lost. Listen to your language - has it lost respect for your people? Do you talk about winning and losing? Time to revisit what you both want and go for a win-win solution.

When *you* are the Brickwall

If you experience being on the opposite side, or talking about 'them and us' - then walls are being built all around you. The danger here is that you begin to think the other side is less worthy than yourselves and does not deserve your respect. You begin finding reasons why you are different rather than acknowledging what is common to both sides. Don't build the wall too high, have a look over - you may see others dismantling and your options opening up.

33. The Cannon Strategy

This is for the 3-D mentality -
Desperate and Dangerously Determined

(Dangerous thoughts lead to dangerous actions – we are what we think!)

This requires collaboration with a willing party to light the fuse. (Beware of the vindictive person who wishes you harm, giving you false directions and heading you straight into a wall, rather than over it.) An example of this in action is the case of a senior person or manager who writes a letter to the chairperson concerned with all that is wrong, then sends it to the newspaper. Leaks such as these are often fuelled by powerful emotions. Rather than achieving long-lasting breakthrough, the individual is simply fired!

When faced with a Brickwall

Occasionally you are faced with an individual who, for whatever reason, has decided to go to war with you or your organisation. Hold back from fighting fire with fire - try and listen, understand and create an opportunity for conciliation. Also - ask the question, *'how is it that this situation occurred in the first place?'* - What can we learn from it?

When _you_ are the Brickwall

Ever felt so angry you want revenge? Have you been on the side of injustice and want people to know how unfair everything is for you? Stop! This feeling of desperation may create more problems for you in the long run and drain you even further. Take a deep breath and ask yourself - honestly, to what extent have I contributed to this situation?

We are, after all, a reflection of our relationships and our feelings. They say something about us. Find out what this is, calm down and more positive options for action will come to you.

34. Running Through

(When all about you is falling apart, hold yourself together)

This combines the qualities of courage and foolhardiness. You need to prepare for the pain of failure and the ecstasy of success, although the painful consequences of both can be long-lasting.

Even when successful, the damage caused to yourself may be considerable, and the debris left behind may trip you up at a future date.

This is not recommended.

Only use this in moments of desperation and as a last resort when all considerations of care have diminished. This occurs in managers who are so blinded by their way of thinking that they are unable to see other alternatives. This becomes a personal quest, and much more time and debate is spent justifying the approach. The actual run-through occurs when the personal quest is threatened.

When faced with a Brickwall

There comes a time when you have listened, shown support, made adjustments and allowances and still the brickwall (resistance) stands firm. Your frustration rises and you decide to use your personal and positional power to run through all obstacles. You may achieve your objective, but it will be superficial and short term. Forcing change out of frustration can cause you and those around you personal damage, resentment, grief, mistrust and anger - and it may take a while to rebuild positive relationships.

When _you_ are the Brickwall

If one day you arrive at work and find many of the familiar things dismantled, removed or falling apart - watch out! This may be as a result of a very determined push at implementing a change without too much consideration as to how people will react. In these cases - it is better to step aside, resist risking getting hurt from the falling rubble. Take your time, change will change again so you'd better get used to it!

35. Give the Wall a Crisis

(Better to work with a crisis than be its victim)

Certain schools of thought recognise this as an effective model for generating change, i.e. purposefully force a major change or create a crisis.

It is, more in practice, a way of justifying the changes that are forced upon organisations, brought about by years of brickwallness or slow response to market forces.

It is very effective, especially for those who rise to challenges or excel when faced with 'fire fight' and survival.

However, the fallout can be considerable, cynicism may increase and it may be years before healthy foundations for positive change can be laid. Implementing major reorganisation for the review of roles, responsibilities and overheads is an example of function following form. This is the wrong way round. Set the direction – then design a structure to support it.

When faced with a Brickwall

Crisis management is one way of keeping those resistant to change on their toes!! If you find yourself lurching from one crisis to the next - stop! What are you not seeing or learning? Plan ahead, look at the trends and learn from past experiences. If things are not going to plan, don't restructure before you reappraise your strategy, sense of direction or priorities. These are the important indicators. Structure to support the strategy, communicate what is important, stop fire fighting and find the source of the fire!

When *you* are the Brickwall

Are you in the middle of a crisis? Don't know where to turn? Unsure of the future? Fearful of losing control? Remember - when you can keep cool when all those around you are losing theirs - you have a good chance of riding out the crisis with a positive outcome for yourself. What's happening around you is transient - it will pass - what's real and permanent is your experience of the moment - the 'now'! Don't be distracted with external happenings - be in touch with what's real, what's important for you - and this will help you decide the right course of action.

36. Go for the Cracks

(Earn the right to challenge - respect others' vulnerabilities)

Every wall has its weaknesses. Be careful to scan and note small changes; this could be due to environmental or situational changes. Paying attention to the brickwork can help you closely identify cracks and openings that may be developing.

A crack or mismatch in the brickwork may indicate a significant weakness. Tapping this could cause the wall to crumble. There are two different approaches here:

1. Spot the weaknesses and apply a sledgehammer. This can be hard work and potentially destructive and risky; for if it is the wrong weak point – you can get weaker and the wall can get stronger.
2. Tap the weakness at the right time and combine this approach with BMA Number 16; the wall may recognise its own discrepancy or weakness, and with little effort it will crumble safely.

This approach requires powerful challenging skills. If they are conducted in a supportive environment with the intention to help, then long-lasting change is possible. If challenged negatively, then years of resentment and mistrust can develop.

When faced with a Brickwall

It might be by listening and getting closer to those who are resisting change that you spot weaknesses or discrepancies in what they are saying and doing. Pointing these out with supportive debate may help them see things differently. Confronting head on may just reinforce the defence.

When *you* are the Brickwall

We all have our weak points. We all feel vulnerable at times. This is one reason we build our own resistance (brickwall) to what we perceive as threatening. However, our reluctance to do something, or our fears and anxieties, are a disguise for significant learning opportunities. Open up a little, see what's there - you might be delightfully surprised!

37. The COWTH Method

Catch Off-guard With Trust and Humour

(You can't buy trust, loyalty and respect)

This is for the highly manipulative and ambitious. The most common method is through wining and dining and having fun, while at the same time gaining information unwittingly from the brickwall. When laughing and relaxing, cracks and openings appear; they may be large enough to walk through.

The advantages

● You can slip through the wall without having anyone realise it if you're highly skilful.
● It avoids direct confrontation.
● You are able to use the same method again with the same wall (however, this may get expensive).

The disadvantages

● If you're found out, this can cause long-term resentment and create enemies. (Watch out for the young walls aspiring toward a non-wall structure – this could be a future powerful foe.)
● For the ambitious with a code of ethics, this may create twinges of guilt.
● If you're using this method on a regular basis, it can turn on you to such an extent that you don't know who your genuine friends are. This can be an acceptable method for those who are mutually politically astute.

When faced with a Brickwall

A great deal of legitimate business is done at the dining table, on the golf course or other social events. The reality of making things happen involves influence and personal power. Whether this is social or at a formal meeting, it is better to have the agenda up front so you see an honest reaction and, therefore, plan accordingly. Manipulation and playing games will eventually back fire and it will be you who loses out.

When *you* are the Brickwall

If you find yourself unexpectedly being wined and dined by someone who usually makes demands on you and is not your normal social choice of partner, then ask yourself - 'what's this about?'

People in power will often use the social occasion to get their point across. They believe the social ambience will lower defences, reduce the likelihood of a reaction and ease any pain associated with the message.

Messages vary from 'you're fired', 'you're changing job', 'I have a special assignment for you' and 'I want your support so you must buck your ideas up'!

Ask yourself before saying yes to the invitation - on whose terms do you want these conversations? Check out the menu first!

38. Threaten the Wall

(Threatening others demonstrates your weakness)

Be sure of your ground when using this method. Be prepared to carry through your actions and understand the implications of using it. Walls are very resilient and resistant to this method.

During the process of threat, this method may build reinforcements to the wall. Even if successful, the walls have an uncanny way of rebuilding, particularly if this method is used.

You can build up a certain reputation using this method, and walls have been known to close ranks, making this method even more difficult.

When faced with a Brickwall

'When the going gets tough, the tough get going' - unless you're on the receiving end of being bullied. Abuse of power is an ego trip that does nothing but create tension, stress and uneasy relationships. Ask yourself why you feel the need to threaten - could it be you feel a little lost as to what else to do? Ask for help, look at alternatives and reflect on the many approaches described here for you.

When *you* are the Brickwall

When under threat it is reasonable to build up that wall, brick yourself in, defend yourself! When you feel safe behind your wall, it may be worthwhile considering what you actually find threatening. No one can take away who you are, your unique talents, your incredible potential and your sense of what's right and what's wrong. At the end of the day, what is feared is loss of material security. If you become secure in yourself and who you are - then material security becomes less important, the threats reduce and if you desire it - material wealth becomes easier but remains secondary to personal inner wealth.

39. Crumble by Humiliation

(The least effective way of feeling sorry for yourself)

- Humiliate and degrade the wall until it crumbles.
- Take every opportunity to highlight negative points.
- Focus on its non-usefulness and its senseless waste of space.
- State with aggressive tone, 'You are a poor excuse for an object!'

This method is particularly useful for those managers who have a poor self-image. It can have the effect of making them feel better by creating someone or something worse than themselves. The reality of this difference must be questioned.

When faced with a Brickwall

Insulting others, criticising them, judging them or belittling them - what do you think that's about? Fundamentally, it's about making you feel better. It's about you feeding your ego (self importance) and positioning yourself as superior. What do you think it achieves? It achieves mistrust, distance in relationship and, potentially, a fearful workforce, demotivated and one that hides mistakes - is this what you want?

When *you* are the Brickwall

'Sticks and stones may break my bones, but names will never hurt me!'

Other peoples' criticism and insults are a reflection of themselves. Sit on your brickwall and smile sweetly - this will not break your defensiveness. Whilst sitting, you could (if you are brave enough) consider what aspect of the insult or criticism may be true, but do it on your own terms, in your own time and not as a response to the one hurling stones.

40. Insight through Popularity and Attention

(Choose when you want to be taken seriously)

This is a risky one! It has been known to backfire and reinforce the opposite effect than intended. On the other hand, it has been known to cause some movement in the wall through doubt and embarrassment. This is done by creating sufficient incongruous attention to the state of brickwallness.

The best chances of success occur when attention is given by those usually known to be genuine and non-game players. If a reputation of being sarcastic is part of any of the 'attention giver's' make up, then the approach may easily be discovered.

Serious debriefing of the wall afterwards may be needed, followed by a good humoured booze-up!

When faced with a Brickwall

Hardly the most open of approaches and you risk the message never being heard or understood - at worst, you may reinforce the behaviour you do not want. Better not to collude and either help the individual on the receiving end of jokes and sarcasm to confront it or model an alternative approach to your colleagues and give the message - treat with respect and support others to change, rather than ridicule or abuse.

When *you* are the Brickwall

Have you ever been on the receiving end of someone else's joke? Ever been the last person to get the punch line? Are you often in a discussion where sarcasm refers to you in some way? You need to decide whether you laugh with them and carry on as you are, or call their bluff - ask, *'what are you really saying?'*, *'what's the real message?'* Be prepared to receive feedback that has probably been building up for some time. This can be a positive experience if you are willing to follow it through.

41. Bribe the Wall

(To bribe is to devalue what you are trying to achieve)

This is a negative use of reward, and a false incentive (i.e. using the external reward as a carrot on a stick).

If you accept, try it out or influence this idea, i.e. 'There's a better car in it for you' – this is devaluing the change required.

Unfortunately, it is often very effective. However, it is usually short lived (about as long as the novelty of a new car), and once the reward (bribe) is given, the commitment to carry through is very weak. It encourages inappropriate learning, and if used excessively, it may diminish many intrinsic motivation factors within the workforce, e.g. self respect, pride, integrity, self-esteem and personal satisfaction.

When faced with a Brickwall

Using rewards to push and encourage staff to go beyond their comfort zone can work, however, it can be equally demotivating especially for most who strive to achieve the target and just fail. These people may be tempted to cheat and it also can create internal negative competition. Better to have an open, transparent and fair reward scheme combined with a positive praise culture.

When *you* are the Brickwall

Being rewarded for good performance is welcome, however, be aware of those rewards offered to encourage you to do things that are inconsistent with the ethics and values of the business. Tempting as it may be - the efforts focussed on reward can increase the occurrence of short cuts, misinterpretation and fiddling the books.

42. Blackmail the Wall

(Colluding with the darkside keeps you in the shadows – eventually to be found out!)

Skills required:

- ✓ research
- ✓ observation
- ✓ stamina to find sufficiently damning material.

Qualities required:

- ✓ ruthlessness
- ✓ little or no guilty conscience
- ✓ lack of care.

Appropriateness

This is hardly ever appropriate. Only if you are desperate to demonstrate commitment to break through, no matter what, is this appropriate. Only then use it as a theoretical example of what you are prepared to do. It is very difficult to justify openly, yet it is amazing how much of this goes on! Usually, it is conducted within the shadows of organisations. (e.g. 'I'll expect your support for this project, unless you want your misappropriation of the firm's equipment discussed at Board level?!')

Consequences

It create enemies for life. Prosecution from police or an internal audit are possible if you are unsuccessful, leaving the wall more determined than ever to maintain the barrier.

When faced with a Brickwall

> Abuse of power, no matter how frustrating someone's resistance is, is not appropriate. Better to have an honest dialogue and explain your frustration.

When _you_ are the Brickwall

> Don't be a victim. Refuse to be intimidated. This is a case where hanging on to what's familiar is needed. You may want to consider whether this is an organisation you want to work for given its approach to managing people.

43. Scare the Wall

(Use the fear and discover the opportunity it creates)

What frightens brickwalls?

Basically, anything that threatens to damage or move them.

For example

✖ **Demolition gangs.** (They present a situation where it is going to happen anyway, so you may as well dismantle or stand aside.)

✖ **Vandals with spray cans and sledgehammers.** (You're going to be abused if you don't give way.)

✖ **Earthquakes.** (The consequences of not moving are earth shattering; they are the 4 Rs – Retraining, Redeployment, Redundancy and Retirement.)

When faced with a Brickwall

Do not underestimate the anxiety and fear caused by announcing impending changes in work conditions. With any announcement of change must come the announcement of support. Regular communication and updates are essential.

When *you* are the Brickwall

If you are experiencing enforced job change, a new boss, change of location, change of system, new demands or image because of a merger or take over - all these can be scary or unsettling. It's good to remind yourself that you can only change those things that you have some control over, in this case - it's your feelings and ability to adapt.

Advanced Approaches

44. Rise Above the Wall

(Be ambitious, but not blind)

This is particularly useful for those who wish to prove a point. High flyers are particularly attracted to this method. They may be misdirected by their own enthusiasm to invest resources into building something that may be seen as just 'hot air'.

Often, the energy of the 'high flyer' causes them to be blind to dangerous environmental factors that are likely to hinder the project's success.

You probably need to link up with an experienced anchor person early, so that the ideas generated are shaped for realistic implementation.

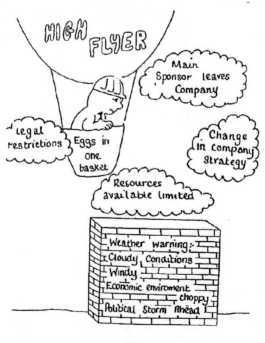

When faced with a Brickwall

It's understandable to want to progress, be successful and be ambitious. It may be that you can seize the opportunity to prove to your boss that you can rise above any obstacle. Remember to occasionally slow down, take in the scenery, acknowledge those on the way who help you, learn from those less agile than you - but steeped in experience - and don't get carried away with your own sense of importance. Maintain some humility as you can always learn. If you aspire to a significant leadership position, then you want to be approachable - yes?

When *you* are the Brickwall

It is sometimes useful to ask yourself what you want out of work. If you find yourself left behind, or surrounded by young high flyers whose energy and enthusiasm creates even more work and pressure for yourself - then perhaps it's time to review where you are and what you want. Without adapting in some way - you will be left behind, only causing resentment and barriers between you and the rest. Swallow your pride; learn from the young high flyers and they will learn from you.

45. Counsel the Wall

(Listen and understand)

Success will be dependant upon:
- ✓ a willing wall
- ✓ a degree of trust from the wall
- ✓ counselling skills.

This is increasingly seen as a vital part of management skill and responsibility.

Inhibitors

- Counselling is often seen as a weakness rather than a strength.
- Its value is usually only recognised by people or walls who have been counselled themselves.

The idea behind this method is to get the wall to dismantle itself in its own time. This method is likely to be permanent and acceptable to all concerned.

This is one of the more effective BMAs. In business terms, it can be seen as initially expensive, but in terms of quality of working life and long-term productivity, it is extremely cost effective.

When faced with a Brickwall

Being trained in basic counselling skills as a manager will increase many of your interpersonal skills. You must, however, recognise that this does not make you a counsellor. If faced with a work colleague with significant problems, by all means listen - but listen out for the appropriate channel for help. Be clear about what referral options you have, e.g. Employee Assistance Programmes (EAP), occupational health, other counselling services or a mediation officer and so on. Know your own limits to help, be clear about your support and expectations for the need to seek help and get 'it' sorted.

When *you* are the Brickwall

Occasionally, in your working life, problems in your personal life affect your performance. This will be visible to those who work with you. It will also make it more difficult to handle change or stress at work. Some organisations offer EAP and confidential counselling services. If you're lucky enough - you may have a boss who is a good listener - this may be enough to see you through. Don't be afraid to ask for help.

46. Gain Rapport, Pace and Lead

(Focus on being with another)

A high degree of brickwall empathy is needed here to be fully aware of the wall-state, and then to mirror and pace its every movement. Once this has been achieved, slowly lead the wall into opening up, or moving, by first moving yourself. This can create a sufficient brickwall shift, allowing the use of other BMAs to produce significant change.

Empathy is that state where you step into another person's shoes and see the world from their perspective. It requires you not to be judgemental and that you not only listen to the words that are spoken, but also the feelings expressed.

When faced with a Brickwall

Listening to people's feelings and concerns is a core leadership skill. Having empathy will enable you to gain rapport and respect. This will give you a foundation to build on and encourage change. Modelling the behaviours you desire from an understanding of your team's position will encourage them to change.

When *you* are the Brickwall

It's easier to change if you are working with people or have a boss that really understands your position. Being able to express your feelings and build a relationship on trust will slowly encourage you to move. If you are fortunate to have this empathy around you - use it, move, change with people - you may find it a rewarding experience.

47. Model Non-Brickwallness

(Be yourself, genuine and honest)

You must be able to demonstrate the following:

- ✓ **Openness** – be open to new ideas and use good listening techniques.
- ✓ **Clarity** – do not hide anything or have a hidden agenda.
- ✓ **Flexibility** – be willing to move from your stand point and accommodate others' differences.
- ✓ **Unblocking** – encourage others to move and invite others to pass through, i.e. genuinely incorporate others' ideas into your own.

Caution

Being too perfect may alienate the wall, as the difference between you and the person or brickwall may be so great that rapport may not be able to be achieved. Gradually build up and, at the same time, show the advantages of non-brickwallness that will help bridge those differences.

When faced with a Brickwall

People in organisations will always look up and observe the behaviours that get rewarded. Whether you like it or not, people will look at you and say - that's how to get on in this organisation. Modelling the behaviours of openness, being genuine and honest and acting out of integrity - will give others a positive role model to look up to.

When *you* are the Brickwall

If you really pay attention to those who seem happy at work and observe what it is they do, you will find that they don't seem fazed or over concerned about new things, or demands made on them, as a result of change. Enquire and ask what motivates them, how do they cope? You may be surprised at their answer. It may be worthwhile trying out their way of working.

48. Love the Wall's Secrets

(There's good in everyone)

Every wall has its secrets. A wall usually is hiding something within itself, as well as standing in the way of things. To the wall, these secrets are often feared; they are uneasy that if the secrets are known, all remaining self-respect will diminish.

It is surprising that what may seem to be a devastating disclosure to some, will often be received and accepted by others. This encourages other disclosures; thus it builds a climate of trust. This is a value expressed by many corporations, yet so many find it difficult to put into practice.

This technique requires forming a relationship with the wall and gaining its trust by trusting it yourself. When its secrets become open, show your acceptance and the wall will give.

When faced with a Brickwall

For some people, it's a big deal to admit fear, anxiety, low confidence or inability to cope with new things. Many think if they disclose their vulnerability, they will be judged as weak. If you can encourage people to open up, perhaps by showing some of your own anxiety and/or vulnerability and then reassuring them that it's okay to be uncertain - you will gain a much more honest assessment of what's going on. Limit your judgement and criticism of others and you will find more people around you to be genuine and real, because they will feel more confident to be themselves.

When *you* are the Brickwall

Some of our fears and anxieties are related to what we have done in the past or what we fear in the future, e.g.

past - guilt, shame, regret and disappointment

future - hope, dreams and doubt.

These feelings or perceptions will prevent you from experiencing the moment. They will distract you from what's happening now and therefore potentially disable you from coping with change. What's in the past or future does not exist - what is real is now. Stop - breathe, experience the moment and celebrate the uniqueness of you. Change won't threaten this.

49. Relaxation Techniques

(Thoughts and feelings can control your heart)

It's surprising how much brickwallness is due to tension, anxiety and insecurity; this causes a great need to tighten up and become rigid. The following techniques are universally effective and, if used regularly, can create an all-round healthier manager.

Some techniques

- use of music
- exercise
- dance
- hypnotherapy
- alternate tension and relaxation
- planned periods of peace (POP) at work
- walks in quiet surroundings
- creation of a soothing work environment with appropriate pictures and colours
- better use of time (the balance between work, home and self).

The author suggested to one company director before a pre-lunchtime meeting:

'Why don't we go for a walk to discuss these issues and get some fresh air and sunshine at the same time?'

The response was, *'No, I don't think so – we don't do that sort of thing here, and besides, people will start talking. It sets a poor example!'*

When faced with a Brickwall

To what extent are you adding to other people's stress at work? If you are stressed, your team will be stressed. To what extent are you creating opportunity for people to de-stress? Take time out, have breaks, do something different. 40 minutes is the average time-span for optimum concentration. After that, without a break, it's down hill. It's amazing how many meetings last for 2 hours or more. No wonder people dread meetings and make bad decisions at the end of them. Have shorter meetings, take more breaks, and create a more relaxed working environment. You will find that it enhances productivity, creativity and efficiency. It may also reduce sick leave!

When _you_ are the Brickwall

As you are reading this, check out your breathing, is it fast or slow? Deep or shallow? Are you frowning or clenching your teeth? What about your hands - are you holding on to the book tightly, tapping your fingers? Shrug your shoulders - do they feel tight? What about your legs - are they crossed, moving - now you will be aware of how tense you are. For whatever reason - tension and stress build up throughout the day. The more stressed you are, the more likely you are to be defensive. Take time out. Relax a little, put things in perspective. Stress eventually will do you in - it's not worth it!

50. Become a Seagull

(If you believe it, you can achieve it)

*'The seagull was demonstrating the elements of high-speed flying...
to avoid a young bird flying in his path, the seagull had to pull up
sharply... he snapped hard to the left, at something over two hundred
miles per hour, into a solid brickwall.'*

Richard Bach, *Jonathan Livingston Seagull*,
London, Pan Books, 1973

It was, for him, as though the wall were a giant hard door into another
world. A burst of fear and shock and black as he hit, and then he was
adrift in a strange sky, forgetting and remembering. He was both
afraid and sad.

The voice came to him as it had on the first day that he had met
Jonathan Livingston Seagull – *'The trick is that we are trying to
overcome our limitations in order, patiently. We don't tackle flying
through rock until a little later in the programme.'*

When faced with a Brickwall

If you set a vision, target or make a proposal that is so far removed from current reality that it becomes difficult to relate to - then people may see it as a 'bridge too far' or a 'step too hard' and, therefore, instead of being inspirational - it becomes demotivating. At least set targets and goals that increase the likelihood of success in the short term - giving you the opportunity to reward and recognise the behaviour you want. Then - you may eventually achieve the 'flying through wall' type breakthrough you are looking for.

When _you_ are the Brickwall

Some things just seem impossible. Sometimes, demands are made upon you that seem totally unreasonable. So much so, that it just makes you stand still and argue the case - that it's okay to do what you're doing, no need to change. Alternatively, you can remind yourself of the significant amount of untapped potential we, as humans, hold. If we believe it - we can do it!

51. Unlearn Defensive Routines

(Let people in, take a risk, learn)

'What makes all this difficult are the programmes and rules that we presently use to deal with threats. Our competencies are based on bypassing, not engaging, defensive routines, on a set of operating assumptions, that are more likely to reinforce the weaknesses and defence of others as well as our own, and on our being in unilateral control and whatever possible – that is, winning rather than losing.'

Chris Argyris, *Strategy, Change and Defensive Routines*
London, Pitman Publishing Ltd, 1985

We need to practise and experiment with new competencies. Design situations where feedback and rich potential for learning exist.

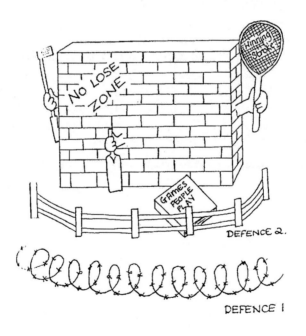

DEFENCE 2.

DEFENCE 1

When faced with a Brickwall

Do not create defensive routines. Avoid easing in to difficult conversations as that may result in confused or mixed messages. Do not confront head on as this will reinforce the brickwall defensiveness. Be clear, objective and business-like. State clearly your observations and expectations and encourage the individual to 'own' the situation (i.e. recognise him- or herself as part of the problem). Maintain a win-win approach in your negotiations and avoid manipulation or playing games.

When _you_ are the Brickwall

We maintain our defences for all sorts of reasons. The purpose of defence is often to buy us time to come to terms with a situation (which is healthy) or argue the case for staying the same (which is unhealthy). Change is inevitable so better to thrive on change rather than resist change and become cynical, negative and potentially depressed and lonely. Be brave, ask for feedback and allow your assumptions to be challenged.

52. Meet a Messiah and Fly

(Be true to yourself)

'Learning is finding out what you already know. Doing is demonstrating that you know it. Teaching is reminding others that they know just as well as you. You are all learners, doers and teachers.

Your only obligation in any lifetime is to be true to yourself. Being true to anyone else or anything else is not only impossible, but the mark of a false messiah.

The simplest questions are the most profound. Where were you born? Where is your home? Where are you going? What are you doing? Think about this once in a while, and watch your answers carefully.'

Richard Bach, *Illusions – The Adventures of a Reluctant Messiah,*
London: Pan Books, 1978

When faced with a Brickwall

If one of your purposes in life is to lead, then it is also to create learning opportunities for those you are leading. The best organisations are learning organisations where managers/leaders know how to coach. Creating an environment where people can achieve their full potential is offering to them an opportunity to be 'a Messiah and fly'.

When _you_ are the Brickwall

Whether you believe in a God or not - there is more to this world than we are capable of realising. Somehow, it is all connected and the miracles of nature and the miracles of being human somehow are taken for granted. Ask yourself - what is your purpose in life? To what extent is your current situation consistent with this? Answering this with an awareness of the many miracles around you will help you become less rigid, less defensive and your barriers or walls will come down.

53. Customer Matching

(Is the customer always right?)

Give the wall the task of defining what a customer is, and what he or she wants.

Ask it to describe a customer stereotype.

Some principles

- ✓ A customer is unique.
- ✓ Every one is different.
- ✓ Customers change from day to day.
- ✓ Their demands and expectations increase.

A wall is no match for the customer. To meet customer requirements, first time, people need to be empowered with authority, job flexibility and a climate of learning and leadership at every level throughout the organisation.

This is the core of achieving a learning culture – one where everyone is committed to continuous improvement and where quality values are expressed with integrity. (See Appendix 1)

By the way – managers = customers = managers = customers. Invariably, you get what you expect.

When faced with a Brickwall

Sometimes, staff lose sight of the core purpose of the business. Reminding staff of the need to be customer-focused, in touch with market forces, trends and expectations will add weight to the case for change, as customers' expectations are forever increasing as technology and wealth work together informing people as to what's possible and available.

When *you* are the Brickwall

No matter what job you are in, you will have a customer, i.e. someone who is on the receiving end of the work that you do. This may be an external customer buying your service or product, or an internal customer, i.e. part of a chain of events in order to eventually make the business work so external customers can be satisfied. Ask yourself - to what extent are you in tune with the changing demands and expectations of your customers? Without customers - no business - no job!

54. Impress with Leadership

(Leaders are vulnerable – why?)

The following is a list of behaviours identified and described by a cross-section of managers at all levels.

A leader:

- gets full commitment from staff, knows their capabilities and encourages and considers their feelings and aspirations

- has strength of purpose and is willing to deal with important issues head on, no matter how tough they are

- does the job for the company and the customer, gives 110% effort and sees self as part of the team

- is open and honest, approachable and dependable, a good listener, and displays interest in other people's points of view

- will take action and has a 'let's go for it' attitude

- will discuss decisions and listen to arguments, and disseminates all relevant information

- inspires confidence and is trustworthy, and communicates clearly how decisions are made

- delegates, demonstrates trust and encourages ownership of problems

- asks for people's ideas and is prepared to be persuaded by logical, relevant discussion

- cares about people and their problems, and is interested on a personal level

- gives realistic objectives with clear criteria and ground rules

- knows what is going on, has a big picture, looks at problems globally and can communicate the company view.

Combine this with vision and direction, then the chances of a brickwall environment being created are minimised.

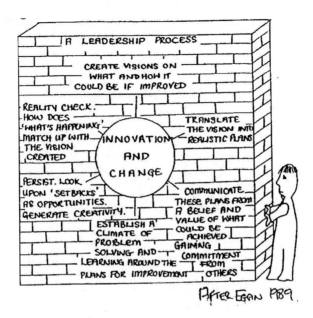

When faced with a Brickwall

> The responsibility of leadership can be far reaching and great. However, the needs of followers are often simple. People need and want honesty, integrity, vision/direction, reassurance that someone cares and is genuinely interested in them as a person who wants to achieve their potential. Do this and loyalty and motivation will be high.

When *you* are the Brickwall

> Whether you like it or not, you are probably a leader. A leader in the sense that what you do influences others. Therefore, the manner in which you do this can shape people's reaction to you. This degree of influence is one aspect of leadership. You can choose to influence positively or negatively. Your attitude to your work can be either a shining example to others or a brickwall. Your choice.

A Practical Exercise to Help You Manage Change at Work More Effectively

Take thirty minutes of uninterrupted time out to do this. If that's difficult, fill in the Time Management Questionnaire in Appendix 1.

STEP 1 – Making sense of it all

So, what's going on?

A. List all the changes that are affecting your work situation at the moment.

B. Include the fears, hopes and rumours.

C. Add the names of the significant people involved.

D. Describe the event(s) that has/have happened which give you cause for concern.

E. What event is about to happen that is likely to create a difference to your work situation?

Example:

A. Changes:

New computer system
New boss
Friend leaving
Team reorganising
Outside consultant
interviewing us

B. Fears, hopes, rumours:

Not enough time to learn the new system, hope I get on with the new boss, it's rumoured that we have lost a major contract and half of us may have to go

C. Who is involved:

(The boss, her boss, my team mates?)

D. Past events:

Workshop where we discussed the new team arrangements.

E. Future event:

Consultant workshop with the new boss

STEP 2 – Taking charge

Okay, so what's your problem? Own up, who didn't include themselves in the list? 'Who's involved in the changes?' **If you are going to manage change, rather than let change manage you, then you need to be clear about what you can influence and what you can't.**

One thing you can influence is YOU; influencing others is more difficult and sometimes not even appropriate.

List those day-to-day activities for which you are responsible.

For example, some general activities are given as a guide. Make your activities as personalised to your situation as possible.

Briefing the team
Sorting the mail
Returning calls
Preparing for meetings
Chairing meetings

Interviewing
Visiting the department
Presenting new developments
Delegating work
Appraising staff

Now describe the changes that will affect you or the changes that you wish to make. Include your issues and concerns related to these.

STEP 3 – What is important?

By now you will have a greater insight into what your concerns or fears are about – changes that are about to take place. However, you can't deal with everything at once, so from the list – can you identify the one thing that, if handled, would have the greatest impact?

For example:

→ If I got on better with the new boss, other positive things would flow from this.

→ This system must be sorted first, as it affects everyone.

→ Managing my time better would really make a difference.

Choosing one area that's important to you, if managed well, makes a significant difference. (Make sure your statement has an 'I' in it. This ensures that you have a degree of ownership for the change you are about to influence.)

STEP 4 – Predicting success

Okay, it's time to change your tempo! You've spent enough time worrying about problems and things that need to be done. Let's test your creative ability. Instead of rushing straight to solutions (which most people do), you will be more effective if you can clearly define what you want! Try and answer the following:

Imagine yourself in a world where problems related to change no longer exist, and you have everything sorted. (See BMA 25)

It may help you to stick to some rules:

✗ No barriers or brickwalls.

✗ No limit of resources.

✗ No personal inhibitions.

Now answer the following and describe the situations problem-free.

What are you doing?	What other activities are going on?
How are you feeling?	Describe the changes around you.
Who else is involved?	Where are you?

Let your imagination run wild and have fun; no one is going to judge you. (Remember this is the WHAT, not the how.)

By now, you should have a rich picture of a future that you ideally would want in terms of the changes being managed. It should feel good!

STEP 5 – Realistic wants

Time to come out of the clouds! Look at future picture and underline those things that could really be achieved. They may still be quite challenging or far from what you have at the moment; however, it's important now to state clearly and specifically the elements of the future you want. So set yourself personal goals.

For example:

→ By the end of this month, I will be proficient in using the basic programmes on our new system.
→ By the twenty-first of this month, I will have communicated effectively my needs and concerns to my boss.
→ Three months from now, I will be managing my time more effectively, i.e. attending meetings on time, not cancelling appointments and going home at five-thirty each evening.

Your personal goals should be SMART:
  ✓ **S**pecific.
  ✓ **M**easurable.
  ✓ **A**chievable.
  ✓ **R**ealistic.
  ✓ **T**ime-framed.

STEP 6 – Testing commitment

Are you prepared for the implications of getting what you want? A way of testing this out is to again remind yourself of the future, in terms of you being successful in managing this change. This time, use the following structure to help.

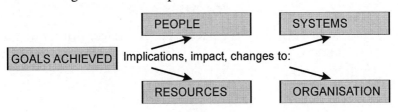

GOALS ACHIEVED — Implications, impact, changes to: PEOPLE, SYSTEMS, RESOURCES, ORGANISATION

Use the above to predict the impact of the change you are likely to create. Use the boxes that make sense for you and ask yourself questions.

For example, concerning PEOPLE

→ Who will be affected?

→ Will there be any changes in roles and responsibilities?

→ Will there be any impact on team work – the way we relate to each other, etc?

Once you have explored what the likely impact of success and change is, and you still want this, then you are ready for the next step.

STEP 7 – How to get what you want

Again, we change pace. This stage requires free thinking and imagination. The number of ideas is important here. The ideas here are about things you can do to achieve your goals. There are at least fifty-four ways of doing anything, so you have a target to aim for! Brainstorm yourself a list of actions you could take to help you achieve your goals. (Remember BMA 30).

This list should include some wild ideas. Have fun with it, for out of the wild ideas, there is usually some amount of action that will be possible, or it may prompt further creativity.

STEP 8 – Choosing actions

Again, reality must have its day. From the list you have generated, underline those things that you think are likely to work – those that sound as if they will make their mark and help you progress toward achieving your goals. Once you have a short list of actions, you have the makings of a plan.

STEP 9 – Planning for success

Whether plans for change are successful or not will depend on the amount of preparation (such as what you have just completed) and the level of detailed planning. All of this contributes to the starting plan and successful follow-through.

For this stage, write down a step-by-step plan, in sequence, i.e.

what you are going to do first, second etc.

Now take the first step. Ask yourself the following questions concerning your first step:

→ What might get in the way of you doing this?

→ What could you do to prevent these things getting in the way?

→ What might help you to be successful in this first step?

→ What things might you do to increase the potency of this?

The answers to these questions will lead you to further detailed thinking and preparation before you implement your plan of action; thus you will minimise the possibility of yourself, or others, sabotaging it.

IF YOU HAVE GOT THIS FAR, YOU ARE NOW MANAGING CHANGE, RATHER THAN CHANGE MANAGING YOU.

This exercise has been adapted from the work of Dr. Gerard Egan. A comprehensive look at change management can be found in *The Skilled Helper*, 4th Edition Brooks/Cole. 1990 and *Change Agent Skills: Managing Innovation and Change*. University Associates. 1991 2nd Edition, both by Dr. Gerard Egan.

Appendix 1

Time Management – Self Assessment

For each question, circle the score that best describes your situation.

		Never	Rarely	Sometimes	Usually	Mostly	Always
1	I know what my activity profile is one week or more ahead	0	1	2	3	4	5
2	I have planned time each day to go through the 'in tray'	0	1	2	3	4	5
3	The time is uninterrupted, except for emergencies	0	1	2	3	4	5
4	I spend at least fifteen minutes at the end of each day reviewing achievements and planning for tomorrow	0	1	2	3	4	5
5	I have some flexibility planned in the day to cater for unforeseen circumstances	0	1	2	3	4	5
6	I am on time for my meetings	0	1	2	3	4	5
7	My meetings start and finish on time	0	1	2	3	4	5
8	Appointments made are fixed (i.e. never cancelled/postponed)	0	1	2	3	4	5
9	My priorities for my job's success are clear to me	0	1	2	3	4	5
10	My priorities for my job's success are clear to my boss	0	1	2	3	4	5
11	My priorities for my life are clear to me	0	1	2	3	4	5
12	My priorities for my life are clear to my family	0	1	2	3	4	5

		Never	Rarely	Sometimes	Usually	Mostly	Always
13	I spend time with my support staff each day reviewing appointments and planning ahead	0	1	2	3	4	5
14	My desk is tidy and relatively paper free	0	1	2	3	4	5
15	If I want some records from my files, they are easily and quickly accessible	0	1	2	3	4	5
16	My telephone calls out are planned and are timed, ie I know what I want to say and achieve	0	1	2	3	4	5
17	My telephone calls are controlled with courtesy and efficiency	0	1	2	3	4	5
18	I work forty hours a week or less	0	1	2	3	4	5
19	I leave work at work; it doesn't come home	0	1	2	3	4	5
20	I get out and see all my staff at least once a week in their work situations	0	1	2	3	4	5
21	I have space in my day for my staff to come and see me	0	1	2	3	4	5
22	My holidays are well planned ahead and agreed with my team	0	1	2	3	4	5
23	I carry minimal paper to meetings	0	1	2	3	4	5
24	At work 100 percent concentration for paper and people is available (ie no daydreaming)	0	1	2	3	4	5
25	Visitors are welcomed at planned times	0	1	2	3	4	5
26	I say 'no' to short-term and unreasonable requests	0	1	2	3	4	5

		Never	Rarely	Sometimes	Usually	Mostly	Always
27	When I delegate a task, I leave them to it	0	1	2	3	4	5
28	I only deal with one thing at a time	0	1	2	3	4	5
29	I stick to the speed limit when I travel from one site to the next in between appointments	0	1	2	3	4	5
30	I make sure there is time in the day for me.	0	1	2	3	4	5

Now total up your score. For a commentary on how well you manage your time see 'Scores' sheet.

Scores

130 -150	Either you should be a Consultant specialising in Time Management or you need to relax a little!
100 – 130	Not bad at all! You seem to have your act together.
70 – 100	Some room for improvement, attention to one or two critical areas may make a significant difference to you and those around you.
Below 70	Boy, do you need help. Slow down, review what's going on. How much fire fighting are you doing – 'Contain the blaze and get to the source'.

Appendix 2
Values for Effective Organisational Change and Improvement

Customer focused
✓ We know who our customers are.
✓ Their requirements are clear and respected.
✓ Our customers are involved in decisions and are concerned with how our product / service is delivered.

Valuing staff
✓ We believe our people are our most important asset.
✓ We recognise the connection between success in Managing Change and the process of empowerment.

Results
✓ Our successes are visible with tangible measures.
✓ We reward achievement using clear criteria.

Openness
✓ We review our actions regularly.
✓ We give feedback to each other freely.

Common language
✓ We use a common approach to Project Management.
✓ We have a common understanding of:
    a. our vision
    b. our mission
    c. our values.

Training
✓ We are committed to training everyone in the organisation in the principles and essential techniques of Change Management.

Learning
✓ We strive to be a learning organisation, in that we coach each other and review continuously to make explicit what we have learnt and the opportunities for improvement.

One Direction
✓ The mission, our roles and responsibilities are all 'lined up' with, and contributing to, the achievement of the vision.

Open Management Styles
✓ Difficult issues and differences are aired and discussed with business objectives in mind.
✓ Politics are brought out of the shadows and dealt with positively.
✓ Managers are accessible and visible.
✓ Status, hierarchy and professionalism cease to be barriers.

Professional Time Management
✓ Time is viewed as a precious resource and hence planned consistently with priorities.
✓ There is appropriate ownership and delegation of problems.

Effective Meetings
✓ This is the most expensive management tool turned into the most efficient, by skilled preparation, facilitation and follow through.

Communication:
✓ There are clear, open, relevant and regular briefings throughout the organisation, quality issues being the main content.
✓ Briefings are consistently conducted with active participation from the recipients – thus creating a two way briefing system.
✓ Internal customer / supplier relationships are clear and contracted service requirements explicit.
✓ Our external customers are regularly informed of:
   a. our activities
   b. our purpose
   c. our achievements
   d. our quality policies.

Team Work:
✓ Teams are structured around customer needs and the core work purpose.
✓ There is a culture of collaborative problem solving, conducted with a high degree of team spirit.

Appendix 3
Guidelines for Designing and Leading Culture Change

The following guidelines are intended for Chief Executives, Senior Managers and organisation development specialists of medium to large organisations.

The phased approach is useful in that it helps plan ahead, checks progress and can shape cultures.

In reality, the phases will overlap and within each phase there are complexities and challenges to be addressed.

These guidelines are based on experiences of introducing this type of programme across different types of organisations. Previous clients of the author who have gone down this path of a phased approach to culture change are:

BT
Aintree Hospitals
York College of Health Studies
Caithness and Sutherland NHS Trust
Nanoquest Instruments
Schools Curriculum Industry Partnership
Volex Wiring Systems
Raydex Cables
Pencon Electronics
Farnell Electronic and Industrial Distributors
United Leeds Teaching Hospitals NHS Trust
Royal Liverpool Children's NHS Trust
Renfrewshire and Inverclyde Primary Care Trust
ABS Wastewater Technology Limited

Phase 1 **AWARENESS**   Top team strength, ambition and awareness

Phase 2 **PREPARATION**   Top team preparation and understanding the implications of culture change and leadership development

Phase 3 **TRAINING**   Top team training, design and prepare for training facilitators and educating all staff

Phase 4 **RECRUIT CHAMPIONS** Involve senior managers, select facilitators

Phase 5 **BREAKTHROUGH**   Train facilitators, put theory into practice to next tier of management

Phase 6 **INVOLVEMENT**   Cascade the process throughout the organisation

Phase 7 **COMMUNICATE AND MEASURE**

Phase 8 **CELEBRATE SUCCESS**

Phase 1 - Awareness

Top team strength, ambition and awareness

1. Introduce your ambition for the organisation.
2. Introduce the idea of using frameworks as a vehicle to achieving excellence, e.g. Investors in People (IIP), Scottish & British Quality Award, European Foundation for Quality Management.
3. Get the basics right.
4. Pragmatic management - financial control.
5. Find a common language for the top team, eg: does everyone have a shared understanding of what strategy means?
6. Build trust, comradeship and teamwork.
7. Create a vision as part of the overall strategy, creating a sense of direction that key players can buy into, i.e. they can see the benefit or pay off.
8. Put great store in people management - manage the top team

performance well and expect them to cascade this.

9. Involve the Chairman and non-executive Directors in an added value role in supporting the strategic agenda.
10. Ask yourself - can this team lead 'transformation'.
11. Bring in data highlighting the percentage of failure activity and its costs within the organisation.
12. Staff survey / diagnostic. Find out what people really think about working in the organisation.

Phase 2 - Preparation

Top team preparation and understanding the implications of culture change and leadership development

1. Top team workshop around the questions:
   a) 'How do we create a continuous improvement culture?'
   b) 'How can we develop a learning organisation?'
2. To do this we need to look at strategy, leadership and team behaviour.
3. We need personal development plans for:
   a) personal style, behaviour change and team contribution
   b) increased knowledge about what it will take to lead transformation.
4. Highlight current internal best practice.
5. Work with key influential players - managers and key professionals. Involve them in early thinking - seek their opinions
6. Devise a robust communication strategy.

Phase 3 - Training

Top team training, design and prepare for training facilitators and educating all staff

1. Design of a culture change process.
2. Basic education for all staff.
3. Process for involving all staff.
4. Change agent or facilitator training.
5. Agree basic tools e.g. project management framework, problem solving, tools and techniques.
6. Address basic training needs in the top team.
7. Meeting and time management training for all managers.

8. Problem solving.
9. Team leadership skills.
10. Further team building needs
11. Top team preparation for launch of culture change.
12. Begin to set up key improvement groups, e.g.: communication, performance management and customer care.
13. Continue to shape up the vision - highlight values - purpose.
14. Ensure key stakeholders are involved.
15. Gain current perceptions from next tier of management about their level of involvement.

Phase 4 - Recruit champions

Involve senior managers, select facilitators

Senior Management (and clinicians or other key professionals, e.g. lawyers, teachers, specialists etc depending on the organisation) involvement.

1. Design basic material for all staff.
2. Select facilitators and design training.
3. *either* presentations/briefing from CE followed by Workshops *or* workshops led by CE and Directors.
   or both.
4. Identify steering group if it's not the top team.
5. Follow up workshops - identify what will work in own unit/dept/ function.

Phase 5 - Breakthrough

Train facilitators, put theory into practice to next tier of management

1. Train your facilitators.
2. Cascade to next tier of management - mixed groups.
3. Add momentum to current improvement groups.
4. Ensure - survey results are directed toward improvement initiatives.
5. Begin to receive proposals from Directors and Senior Managers as to how the change process could be adapted to work in own 'patch' or department.

Phase 6 - Involvement

Cascade the process throughout the organisation

1. Match facilitators with Director and Senior Management improvement plans.
2. Design in events to keep the momentum going e.g. Chief Executive Awards scheme, special newsletter.
3. Check on integration of the new way of working into induction, appraisal, training, selection procedures.
4. Design database to capture and communicate progress and learning from the many improvement initiatives and projects.
5. Encourage the cascade supported by Senior Managers (and Clinicians) with presentations by CE and Directors.
6. Form 'bottom-up' Quality Action teams around local improvement initiatives.

Phase 7 - Communicate and measure

1. Communicate, communicate, communicate!
2. Make the links between tangible improvements and the new way of working.
3. Go for some form of recognition e.g. National Quality Award.
4. Measure, measure, measure!
5. Transform the way notice boards, displays and walls will look.
6. Ensure that customer feedback is considered when reviewing progress.
7. Encourage benchmarking

Phase 8 - Celebrate success

1. Re-launch the programme e.g. hold a 'Quality Day'.
2. Get the media involved.
3. Re-survey staff, customers and patients.
4. Market the results!!!
5. Stress the importance of keeping going - this is a continuous journey - not a destination - as you turn one corner, or achieve one milestone the horizon changes - better performance is always possible.

Appendix 4
Rate your Team against the Best Characteristics of the Excellent Top Team

Support

Listening and challenging each other's strengths. Building on each other's positive achievements. Doing that bit extra for each other when one of the members is out of action or preoccupied. In the public domain, speaking with one voice; privately, not holding back on an honest expression of views.

Understanding

Personal   each others' situation, hopes, aspirations and personal circumstances

Team   valuing the role and contribution each makes

Organisation showing insight and appreciation of each others function and work related challenges.

Corporateness

Legal, ethical and social responsibility and accountability understood and collectively owned.

Each having an ability to communicate the total picture of the organisation and the rationale for its greater value than its parts.

A strong sense of identity and associated pride.

Communication

Knowing what to say, when and how much. Not taking each other for granted or making assumptions. Consciously carrying each other around, listening for each other, providing rich and relevant 'intelligence'.

Enthusiasm

Genuine commitment to the value of working as a team. Higher energy evident when working together.

Synergy
Unique and creative contribution evident when team performs well.

The combination of individual talent and strengths begin to show through lateral thinking, new situations, innovation and new learning.

Stability
Knowing where you stand with each other.

At least – an honest expression of intention of own future and ambitions at this current moment in time.

At best – a team commitment for a set period (get out clause permissible). Worthwhile targets for organisation achievement and recognition set.

Self Team Assessment

Write down your perception of your team now

	Weak			Strong	
Support	1	2	3	4	5
Understanding	1	2	3	4	5
Corporacy	1	2	3	4	5
Communication	1	2	3	4	5
Enthusiasm	1	2	3	4	5
Synergy	1	2	3	4	5
Stability	1	2	3	4	5

Appendix 5
Managing Effective Meetings

A meeting is the most expensive way of communicating, problem-solving and/or making decisions in terms of the time spent in them. It therefore seems reasonable that we do the utmost to ensure the preparation, design and conduct of these meetings are appropriate and successful.

Managing effective meetings

Some key principles

- It is reasonable to expect to be told what the purpose of any meeting is.
- It is good management practice to communicate the purpose of any meeting and expectations of individuals you invite to a meeting.
- The clearer you are on the 'outcome' you are looking for, the more support you get in achieving this.
- The organisation benefits from training managers and key people in meeting management skills by improving:
  - *effectiveness* – ensuring the meeting focuses on the right issues
  - *efficiency* – through optimum use of time.

Effective meetings will:

- have an agenda influenced by the participants
- deal with the important issues as well as the urgent
- deal with strategic and development issues as well as operational issues
- work with explicit values such as openness, trust, honesty, equal participation
- reach outcomes whereby responsibility for action is appropriately owned.
- be accurately, but not over, recorded.
- be enjoyable and add value.

The following guidelines are offered here to enable good agenda design principles to be applied in the preparation and conduct of meetings.

Meeting management proforma

Time	Title	Purpose and/or outcome	Process	Owner	Preparation	Action

Details for the proforma

Meeting – Give the meeting an identity that is clear. It's amazing how many steering groups, directors and operations meetings there are.

Venue – How many of us have turned up at the wrong place or are rushing around asking where the meeting is at the last minute?

Role clarification – The contract between chairperson and facilitator (if present) is usually clarified well beforehand whilst designing the agenda. Other roles such as minute or note taker and presenters are all part of preparing the ground.

Time – Start and finish time needs to be clear and promptly adhered to. Otherwise significant waste (cost) is incurred, e.g. waiting for people to start. If finish times are not stated or adhered to, then time management and planning for everything else is affected.

Timing agenda items – This is one of the most difficult aspects and challenges for the person who is putting the agenda together – to think through clearly and exactly what this is trying to achieve and how it will be managed during the meeting. It also communicates to the rest of the group the degree of debate or emphasis the agenda item warrants from the owner's perception.

The timings are usually an indicator only and some flexibility is usually called for.

Agenda Items – Clarify identity of the topic by name.

Purpose – State why the agenda item is on, e.g.
- to agree
- to discuss/debate
- to give information
- to identify causes of particular problems
- to gain ownership/commitment
- to increase understanding
- to take stock of progress
- to develop plans/thinking
- to introduce new ideas/concepts
- to propose new policy/project

Owner – One or two persons initials needs to be against each item to indicate who has greatest stake or vested interest in this item being discuss. They may also be the person to lead the discussion.

Process – The most neglected area in agenda design. Most agendas consist of lists of items for discussion. This section invites agenda designers to vary the way agenda items are handled. This respects the fact that most of us have an optimum attention span of 40 minutes, and need to do something different, if our concentration is going to be 100%. Many meetings are organised for more than 2 hours, this probably means that key decisions are made when individuals are at their least effective. There must be other ways to achieve the purpose of an agenda item, other than information giving and/or discussion – some could include:

- brainstorm
- cause and effect analysis (or use some other technique)
- presentation
- small group discussion and present back
- individual reflection and present back with a question
- brainstorm questions and choose top/critical three
- feedback key issues from individuals pre-reading of
- relevant papers
- structured problem solving
- open negotiation
- … and I am sure there are many other creative ways of getting people's contribution and participation.

Outcome – This can also be useful, particularly if one of the agenda items is broad or complex. Focusing down on what is expected in terms of the following:

- decision about . . .
- problem solved about . . .
- clarity about . . .

This aspect is often left to the chairperson to summarise as the meeting progresses in terms of 'has the purpose been achieved and what is the related action?'

Preparation – This is useful, especially if pre-reading of relevant papers is required. It is very difficult to read and do justice to a paper presented during a meeting. Also, by encouraging individuals to think about each item, they can then come prepared to contribute or offer relevant data/information they have gathered before the meeting. It does require the agenda to be sent out with sufficient time for meeting members to consider.

Action – This section can be left blank and offered as a section for individuals to record action related to each item as the meeting progresses.

Review of Meeting – Using new techniques and developing a learning organisation are both important aspects of continuous improvement. Feedback can occur for each meeting if a standing item for say 10 – 15 minutes at the end, focusing on how well the meeting went in terms of:

a) content – did we achieve our objectives and stick to the agenda?

b) interaction – how well did we listen, question and participate?

c) process – how well was it chaired and/or facilitated? Did the agenda format work and are there any other ways we could improve the way we meet?

Agenda for Divisional Directors' Meeting

Time	Title	Purpose	Owner	Process	Preparation	Action
3.00pm	Minutes of the previous meeting	To agree accuracy	BR	Ask and respond to feedback	Read before meeting	
3.05pm	Update issues	Update on Leeds Review	BR	Information giving and discussion		
3.10pm	Achievement through Cooperation	To assess progress	MW/BR	Each Director to report on the situation		
3.25pm	Financial Situation	General Update	AM	Giving information		
3.45pm	New income		AM	Consideration of the attached	Read before meeting	
4.10pm	Internal trading	To discuss what is practical in immediate future	BR	BR to lead discussion		
4.30pm	Review	To agree actions and check on value of meeting	MW	MW to facilitate		

Communication Project – Full participation of staff sub-group

Time	Title	Purpose	Owner	Process	Preparation	Action
12.00 – 12.05	Introductions	To welcome new members to the Group	Lindsey	Go round room saying who we all are (as before)	None	
12.05 – 12.55	Group Vision	To shape a future vision for staff participation	Lindsey	Brainstorming and discussion facilitated by Colin	To ask yourself, how will staff partici-pate in the organisation fully in future? What will it be like?	
12.55 – 1.20	Group purpose and objectives	To agree the groups' purpose and the objectives for our work	All, led by Colin	Discussion and writing up ideas on flipchart	To read the previously circulated paper on our purpose	
1.20 – 1.30	Review of meeting and future dates	To find out how we all feel about the meeting, to see if they need improving and to agree future dates for the next 6 – 8 months.	Colin / Lindsey	Each person to say whether this meeting has met their expectations	Please bring your diaries!	

Trustwide COmmunication Group Meeting

Time	Title	Purpose	Owner	Process	Preparation	Action
11.3	Notes from last meeting	Update on a) Rapid communication b) Stakeholder Management	MW	Information giving Review and revise list appropriately Identify any other issues to be considered	Read notes from last meeting	
		c) Other Trustwide issues	AT			
11.45	Internal Communication	Update on progress	MW	Summary paper submitted for information		
12	Stuart briefing Trustwide	To inform group of sessions arranged	AT	Open discussion to clarify purpose of sessions		
12.25	Review meeting	Agree key items for next meeting. Review membership.	MW			

Effective meeting management questionnaire

If all members of a group that meets regularly indicated their rating on each of the elements below, then they all shared these results, this will give a clear indication of where meeting improvement needs to occur.

The Effectiveness of our Meetings

		1 Strongly disagree	2 Disagree	3 Agree	4 Strongly agree
1	Our meetings start and finish on time	☐	☐	☐	☐
2	The agenda is sent out in good time	☐	☐	☐	☐
3	I have ample opportunity to influence the agenda	☐	☐	☐	☐
4	Each agenda item is timed	☐	☐	☐	☐
5	We give sufficient time to each agenda item	☐	☐	☐	☐
6	The meeting is one where my views are welcomed	☐	☐	☐	☐
7	I have no problems challenging a member of the group	☐	☐	☐	☐
8	My views are listened to and respected	☐	☐	☐	☐
9	I participate freely and equally	☐	☐	☐	☐
10	Questions are open with very few hidden agendas	☐	☐	☐	☐
11	I am confident the whole picture is given when appropriate	☐	☐	☐	☐
12	There is very little holding back in our meetings. We say what we think.	☐	☐	☐	☐
13	We are good at bottoming issues out	☐	☐	☐	☐
14	I am clear about how we make decisions	☐	☐	☐	☐

		1 Strongly disagree	2 Disagree	3 Agree	4 Strongly agree
15	When needed, we are able to make decisions by consensus	☐	☐	☐	☐
16	I am relaxed and confident during the meetings	☐	☐	☐	☐
17	I look forward to our meetings	☐	☐	☐	☐
18	Action points are summarised and agreed either during or at the end of our meetings	☐	☐	☐	☐
19	The minutes are an accurate record of the meeting	☐	☐	☐	☐
20	The chairman helps the group to keep on relevant issues	☐	☐	☐	☐
21	Conflict is managed well	☐	☐	☐	☐
22	There is appropriate contribution from everyone, without domination from one or two	☐	☐	☐	☐
23	We meet frequently enough	☐	☐	☐	☐
24	Our meetings are long enough	☐	☐	☐	☐
25	I am clear about the role of each group member	☐	☐	☐	☐
26	I am clear about what is expected of me in each meeting	☐	☐	☐	☐
27	The proportion of time we spend on strategic and operational issues is appropriate	☐	☐	☐	☐

Appendix 6
The Vulnerability of Leadership and Leadership Skills Questionnaire

Leadership is probably the most researched area of management development, yet the practice of improving leadership skills and behaviours seems to be still much in its infancy.

If one did a survey in most companies, and asked the employees: to what extent do they feel they are achieving their full potential or to what extent are they utilising their skills appropriately, the result is probably predictable. That is in the negative. This being the case, then it is surprising that so many companies seem to be slow to recognise that the potential for growth and efficiency lay in the hands and the ideas of their own people. This release of uninhibited excitement and drive to improve one's own output from the workforce is largely dependent on the managers of the organisation creating an environment by which leadership at every level can be realised. However, because our organisations are structured, in the traditional hierarchical sense, this change will have to be modelled from the top.

I wonder how many of you reading this, whether you are a Managing Director, Chief Executive, Middle Manager or Supervisor, can actually answer the following questions:

On a scale of 1 to 5, (1 being strongly disagree and 5 being strongly agree) rate your responses to the following statements:

1. I am seen as very approachable by my staff.

2. They perceive me as a good listener.

3. They learn a considerable amount from me by the way I manage the business.

4. They recognise me as one who will accept them and

understand them as a person as well as a work unit.

5.   We review regularly our meetings, strategy and the direction we are going.

6.   There are very few non-discussable issues in our team meetings.

7.   I welcome feedback about my performance, management style and decision making and people management abilities from my people.

8.   My team know exactly where they stand in terms of what I think of them in relation to their ability, performance and potential.

9.   My team and I understand and are aware of the impact of our behaviour on shaping organisational values, attitudes, and hence performance.

10.   I challenge myself on the assumptions and judgements I hold, particularly those that are likely to influence major decisions.

Add your score up.

If you score top marks, 35 – 50, then Congratulations. You are either living out of leadership values or are kidding yourself in terms of how you really are seen. I would advise you to definitely check out your self perception with the perception of your staff; that is – get them to fill in the same questionnaire focused on you.

If you scored between 25 – 35, I think clearly you have some room for improvement, your strengths and weaknesses are probably known to you and you are probably attempting to be seen to be open to personal change and development. It would be important for you to build on a success and in some pragmatic way, demonstrate your change.

If you have scored in the lowest bracket: 0 – 25, then you either need some serious help, you do not recognise the value of this particular style of working or you are underestimating your performance in these areas.

By demonstrating your openness to feedback, the chances of creating an environment for learning, and hence continuous improvement at the top of an organisation, is increased. It is important to make this learning culture visible by helping individuals formulate personal development plans consistent with behavioural change that is likely to achieve the main aims of the organisation/department. If this is achieved, then it is just possible that you may be able to achieve leadership at every level.

Leadership can also mean loneliness, isolation and vulnerability. To stand up and state clearly one's views on strategy, direction and policy and do so in a way that invites questions and debate, needs a certain degree of courage. It's also a risk in terms of being seen as not having all the answers, not having a magic wand and being open for your views to be challenged. This can be difficult, especially when you are faced with a team or workforce who are looking up and are used to being dependent and expect their problems to be solved for them, rather than having to think for themselves.

Some managers will thrive on this relationship of dependency, it is a great buzz to be in control, to be wanted and needed, yet a measure of successful leadership is not in terms of how much you are needed, nor the ability to control or the degree of dependency you create – it is actually the reverse.

A measure of good leadership is in terms of how well the business runs without you – therefore giving the Managing Directors and Chief Executives time to manage the positive politics, the stakeholders, the networking and the blue sky thinking required in order to take the company into the future.

Lastly, we all enjoy the trimmings of status, but I wonder how many managers are using status as a barrier or as an advantage. To use it as an advantage, one would have to understand the extent of one's own personal power and be aware and conscious of the importance of statements, mannerisms and reactions to issues, discussions and debate in all situations. Using it as a barrier involves being separate, aloof and not feeling the need to justify decisions made.

Leadership is a complex concept but usually involves some fundamental principles related to knowing oneself pretty well and having the capacity to know others. I call this 'Empathetic Leadership', which essentially conveys the need to build trust with those around you and listen at all levels, i.e.

Leadership listening at the:

	future
Strategic level	predictions, trends
	politics
	stakeholders
Management level	all team members
Operational level	keep in touch with workforce
Market level	what the customers are saying
Level of self	reflect, learn, develop, listen to family and friends

Finally, I believe there remains a level of leadership rarely researched or written about. A level which defies definition yet when in discussions over a drink, in a relaxed or reflective mood, many in a leadership position admit to wanting to make a difference, to contribute beyond business results. They see themselves carrying a personal mission that impacts others lives in such a way that connections of real value turn into long lasting supportive relationships. The world of 'Spiritual Leadership' is one few will openly admit to yet I perceive many top managers who carry an aura of respect, drive, commitment and self assurance and are able to see coincidences, affect the energy levels in individuals and groups, and offer significant contribution to the biography of the organisation they are currently with. Many do this unconsciously, and it is here I believe a great untapped area of development remains. I predict within the next ten years the spiritual dimension of leading people in organisations will be as discussable as strategic and team leadership is now.

Leadership Skills Questionnaire

This questionnaire is designed to help you assess your strengths and weaknesses on a number of leadership skills.

On the following pages, you will be given a number of leadership behaviours. You will be asked to rate yourself on these skills, on a scale of 1 - 5. A score of 1 indicates your lowest rating; a score of 5 indicates your highest rating.

You should rate yourself by circling the appropriate number on this scale, e.g.

'Listening to others effectively' (LOW) 1 2 3 4 5 (HIGH)

If you feel that you are very good at listening to others, you should circle '5'.

By completing this self-assessment, you should be able to identify your own strengths and weaknesses. This will allow you to focus on areas which may need attention, both during this workshop and back in the workplace.

All the information collected will be for your own benefit, so we would ask you to complete it as accurately as possible.

Once you have completed your self assessment, complete another assessment; this time based on your knowledge, observation and perception of a colleague. Again, the more honest the assessment, the more valuable it is.

(Approximate completion time = 5 - 10 minutes)

© Michael Wash
University of Leeds

Quality Leadership Skills - Self-evaluation

Please consider the following list and rate YOURSELF on each skill, by circling the appropriate number on the scale 1 -5.

	LOW			HIGH

A) Listening to others effectively.   1 2 3 4 5

B) Reflecting back what others have said to
   check understanding.   1 2 3 4 5

C) Asking open questions.   1 2 3 4 5

D) Challenging what people have said in a
   constructive, non-threatening way.   1 2 3 4 5

E) Giving appropriate, on-going feedback to others.   1 2 3 4 5

F) Acknowledging and praising what others do and say. 1 2 3 4 5

G) Recognising and valuing the strengths and
   potential in others.   1 2 3 4 5

H) Recognising and valuing your own strengths
   and potential.   1 2 3 4 5

I)   Always being open to learning from staff.   1 2 3 4 5

J) Having a clear process for making decisions,
   which is logical and effective.   1 2 3 4 5

K) Communicating your plans and objectives clearly. 1 2 3 4 5

L) Communicating up-to-date and relevant
   information to others.   1 2 3 4 5

M) Communicating your own direction and vision
   to others.   1 2 3 4 5

N) Being clear about your own job and responsibilities. 1 2 3 4 5

O) Taking ownership and responsibility for your own job. 1 2 3 4 5

P) Demonstrating commitment to issues by taking action. 1 2 3 4 5

Q) Working well within a team.   1 2 3 4 5

R) Making myself available to others and giving
   them enough of my time.   1 2 3 4 5

S) Delegating work appropriately.   1 2 3 4 5

Quality Leadership Skills - Colleague evaluation

Please consider the following list and rate A COLLEAGUE on each skill, by circling the appropriate number on the scale 1 -5.

	LOW	HIGH
A) Listening to others effectively.	1 2 3 4 5	
B) Reflecting back what others have said to check understanding.	1 2 3 4 5	
C) Asking open questions.	1 2 3 4 5	
D) Challenging what people have said in a constructive, non-threatening way.	1 2 3 4 5	
E) Giving appropriate, on-going feedback to others.	1 2 3 4 5	
F) Acknowledging and praising what others do and say.	1 2 3 4 5	
G) Recognising and valuing the strengths and potential in others.	1 2 3 4 5	
H) Recognising and valuing your own strengths and potential.	1 2 3 4 5	
I) Always being open to learning from staff.	1 2 3 4 5	
J) Having a clear process for making decisions, which is logical and effective.	1 2 3 4 5	
K) Communicating your plans and objectives clearly.	1 2 3 4 5	
L) Communicating up-to-date and relevant information to others.	1 2 3 4 5	
M) Communicating your own direction and vision to others.	1 2 3 4 5	

N) Being clear about your own job and responsibilities. 1 2 3 4 5

O) Taking ownership and responsibility for your own job. 1 2 3 4 5

P) Demonstrating commitment to issues by taking action. 1 2 3 4 5

Q) Working well within a team. 1 2 3 4 5

R) Making myself available to others and giving
them enough of my time. 1 2 3 4 5

S) Delegating work appropriately. 1 2 3 4 5

SCORES

80 - 95   I suspect you have a slightly inflated opinion of your own ability - check it out!

70 - 80   You are an excellent communicator and personal organiser of priorities. You delegate well, and work effectively within the team. People recognise you as supportive, and can always rely on you for feedback. An effective leader.

50 - 70   A competent communicator and team worker most of the time. You are likely to have your good and bad days. Generally, scoring well in most areas, I suspect you have a number of weaknesses and these, no doubt, will affect other categories. By identifying the circumstances in which these weaknesses become apparent, it may be possible to design a development plan to strengthen them.

38 - 50   You lack confidence in many areas. Seek out objective data and build on your strengths. Identify the areas you feel are the most important and ask for assistance to design opportunities to improve these.

19 - 38   You probably survive by not working with people! You are isolated, or the job does not warrant people skills. Either that or you need serious help in boosting your self-image!

And Finally ...
Am I a Leader?

Do you care about others
Are you willing to give them time
Can you get angry about the failure
And waste caused by crime?
Do you have a passion to make a difference
Can you help others see another option
Are you prepared to make a stance
And communicate clearly your position
Standing boldly stating what's possible
And excite those around you,
Who in turn you inspire
To work beyond the ordinary
With passion, zeal and fire.
Can people read you and your values
Know what you stand for
See your bold and good intent
So they can rely on your candour.
Do you seek out opportunities to learn
From your own and indeed others mistakes
Thriving on new knowledge and yearn
For the opportunity to release the breaks
On people's potential so they can grow
From the seeds you sow.
Can you cry about other's pain
Shout about injustice
Guard against false fame
And listen carefully in case you miss
The wisdom of others.
Do you put into practice
Those values you hold dearly
Those principles you preach

Those behaviours you desire
And those standards you hope to reach.

Can you reflect on your day
And admit to learn
That maybe another way
May lead you to earn
The respect of others who say
We have ideas too
If you let us follow through
And do
For you
To
Achieve extraordinary results
That reflect the spirit and pride
You often hide
Until the applause and roar
Of success are so evident
You may as well sit back and enjoy the ride.
Leaders are big, leaders are small
Leaders don't always walk tall
Quite often they talk with their actions
Quite often they speak with knowledge
And confidence that within a fraction
They can and will take themselves to the edge
Of the unknown to achieve that bit extra
So others learn and benefit
From the legacy of a unique contribution
That makes a difference.
If deep down, these qualities highlighted here
Stir with recognition and instil
That sense of purpose to be true
To an ideal and way of being
Then yes,
Perhaps this is you.

Mike Wash

About the Author

Mike Wash has a Master's Degree in Business and Economics and combines his academic background with years of work experience as a teacher of psychology, Senior Nurse Tutor and a Counsellor within the Health Service. He has had numerous encounters with organisational resistance to change and has used all these resources to enable him to learn how to effectively deal with it. Transferring his knowledge to the commercial sector, he became Principal Consultant for British Telecom, where he implemented programmes to aid individuals and teams cope with the consequences of change in the work place.

In addition to his Master's Degree, Mike also holds a Diploma in Psychology and Certificates in Education. These qualifications have helped to successfully develop his career from a professional psychiatric nurse and counsellor to business consultant.

In 1989, he launched his own business, MWA Quality Consultants. He now consults world-wide on a number of consultancy and training issues from Strategic Top Team Building to raising awareness and developing people so they can handle the severity of crisis. He has a reputation for confronting change at the most senior levels and supporting the development of 'the learning organisation' world-wide.